Microsoft Windows Server 2008 Active Directory Configuration

Lab Manual

WILEY

EXECUTIVE EDITOR   John Kane
EDITORIAL ASSISTANT   Jennifer Lartz
DIRECTOR OF MARKETING AND SALES   Mitchell Beaton
PRODUCTION MANAGER   Micheline Frederick
PRODUCTION EDITOR   Kerry Weinstein
DEVELOPMENT AND PRODUCTION   Custom Editorial Productions, Inc.

To order books or for customer service, please call 1-800-CALL WILEY (225-5945).

ISBN 978-0-470-22508-0

Printed in the United States of America

10 9

CONTENTS

1. **Exploring the Windows Server 2008 Interface   1**

Project 1.1: Modifying Basic Server Settings 3

Project 1.2: Configuring TCP/IP Settings 6

Project 1.3: Configuring a Second Windows Server 2008 Computer (Optional) 8

Project 1.4: Configuring a Windows Server 2008 Server Core Computer (Optional) 11

Lab Review Questions 14

Lab Challenge 1.1: Verifying Active Directory SRV Records 14

2. **Installing Active Directory Domain Services   15**

Project 2.1: Installing the Active Directory Domain Services Role 18

Project 2.2: Installing a New Forest and Domain 19

Project 2.3: Verifying SRV Record Creation 22

Project 2.4: Creating User Accounts for Lab Use 23

Project 2.5: Installing a Child Domain 26

Project 2.6: Verifying Child Domain SRV Records 31

Project 2.7: Installing a Read-Only Domain Controller (Optional) 32

Project 2.8: Installing a Server Core Domain Controller (Optional) 41

Lab Review Questions 45

Lab Challenge 2.1: Verifying That the Kerberos SRV Record Exists for the Child Domain 45

3. **Working with Active Directory Sites   47**

Project 3.1: Replication Management 51

Project 3.2: Preparing Your Infrastructure 56

Project 3.3: Configuring a Site 59

Project 3.4: Configuring a New Subnet 60

Project 3.5: Moving Computers and Creating Site Links 62

Lab Review Questions 65

Lab Challenge 3.1: Configuring Preferred Bridgehead Servers for Sites 65

Lab Challenge 3.2: Making the Even-Numbered Computer a Global Catalog Server 66

Post-Lab Cleanup 66

4. **Global Catalog and Flexible Single Master Operations (FSMO) Roles   69**

Project 4.1: The Global Catalog and the Windows Server 2008 Domain Functional Level 72

Project 4.2: Enabling Universal Group Membership Caching 76

Project 4.3: Working with Flexible Single Master Operations Roles 78

Lab Review Questions 81

Lab Challenge 4.1: Using the DNS
   Console to Verify Global Catalog
   Records on the DNS Server 81
Lab Challenge 4.2: Verifying FSMO
   Role Holders with DCDIAG 82
Lab Challenge 4.3: Determining
   Whether an Attribute Is Replicated
   in the Global Catalog 82

Troubleshooting Lab A   83

5. Creating and Managing Users and

Groups   87

Project 5.1: Creating Administrative
   Accounts 89
Project 5.2: Testing Administrative
   Access 93
Project 5.3: Configuring Groups and
   Permissions 96
Project 5.4: Using dsadd to Add a User
   Account 99
Lab Review Questions 100
Lab Challenge 5.1: Using dsadd to Add
   a User Account to the Users
   Container 101
Lab Challenge 5.2: Changing the UPN
   Suffix with LDIFDE 101

6. Employing Security Concepts   103

Project 6.1: Using Naming Standards
   and Secure Passwords 106
Project 6.2: Employing Administrator
   Account Security 107
Project 6.3: Delegating Administrative
   Responsibility 109
Lab Review Questions 114
Lab Challenge 6.1: Using dsmove 114
Lab Challenge 6.2: Moving Objects
   with ADMT 115

7. Exploring Group Policy

Administration   117

Project 7.1: Configuring the Local
   Computer Policy 120
Project 7.2: Configuring Processing
   Order 123
Project 7.3: Configuring Priority
   Order 126

Project 7.4: Using Block Policy
   Inheritance and Enforce 128
Project 7.5: Using Group Policy
   Loopback Processing 130
Lab Review Questions 132
Lab Challenge 7.1: Disabling the
   Shutdown Event Tracker 132
Lab Challenge 7.2: Hiding Last
   Logged-on Username 133
Post-Lab Cleanup 133

8. Managing Users and Computers

with Group Policy   135

Project 8.1: Configuring Account
   Policies 137
Project 8.2: Configuring Audit
   Policies 140
Project 8.3: Configuring Folder
   Redirection 143
Project 8.4: Enabling Disk Quotas 144
Lab Review Questions 146
Lab Challenge 8.1: Configure a Fine-
   Grained Password Policy 146
Post-Lab Cleanup 147

Troubleshooting Lab B   149

9. Software Distribution   155

Project 9.1: Deploying Software to
   Users 157
Project 9.2: Using Software Restriction
   Policies 160
Lab Review Questions 164
Lab Challenge 9.1: Restricting Access
   to Cmd 164
Post-Lab Cleanup 165

10. Controlling Group Policy   167

Project 10.1: Deploying Software to
   Users 169
Project 10.2: Using Security Filtering
   173
Project 10.3: Working with WMI
   Filters 175
Lab Review Questions 177
Lab Challenge 10.1: Applying WMI
   Filtering 177
Post-Lab Cleanup 178

11. Disaster Recovery and Maintenance 181

   Project 11.1: Installing a Replica Domain Controller 183
   Project 11.2: Resolving Replication Issues 185
   Project 11.3: Performing a System State Data Backup 188
   Project 11.4: Compacting the Database 190
   Project 11.5: Performing an Authoritative Restore 192
   Lab Review Questions 194
   Lab Challenge 11.1: Restoring a User Account 194
   Post-Lab Cleanup 195

12. Configuring Name Resolution and Additional Services 197

   Project 12.1: Installing a New Active Directory Domain 199
   Project 12.2: Creating a Reverse Lookup Zone 201
   Project 12.3: Configuring Secondary Zones and Zone Transfers 202

   Project 12.4: Installing the Rights Management Service Role 204
   Lab Review Questions 206
   Lab Challenge 12.1: Creating a CNAME Record 206
   Post-Lab Cleanup 207

13. Configuring Active Directory Certificate Services 209

   Project 13.1: Installing Active Directory Certificate Services 211
   Project 13.2: Configuring Certificate Revocation 213
   Project 13.3: Configuring Certificate Templates 215
   Project 13.4: Configuring Certificate Enrollment 218
   Project 13.5: Configuring Key Archival and Recovery 222
   Lab Review Questions 226
   Lab Challenge 13.1: Configuring EFS Certificates 227
   Post-Lab Cleanup 227

Troubleshooting Lab C 231

LAB 1
EXPLORING THE WINDOWS SERVER 2008 INTERFACE

This lab contains the following projects and activities:

Project 1.1   Modifying Basic Server Settings

Project 1.2   Configuring TCP/IP Settings

Project 1.3   Configuring a Second Windows Server 2008 Computer (Optional)

Project 1.4   Configuring a Windows Server 2008 Server Core Computer (Optional)

Lab Review Questions

Lab Challenge 1.1   Verifying Active Directory SRV Records

BEFORE YOU BEGIN

Lab 1 assumes that setup has been completed as specified in the setup document and that your computer has connectivity to other lab computers and the Internet. To perform all projects in Lab 1, you will need:

- Two (2) full installations of Windows Server 2008
- One (1) Server Core installation of Windows Server 2008

For subsequent labs, optional projects are provided that involve a second server running the full GUI version of Windows Server 2008 to be configured as a Read-Only Domain Controller and a third server running Windows Server 2008 Server Core. You can use multiple physical computers, or you can use Microsoft Virtual PC or Virtual Server to install and run multiple servers on a single machine. This manual assumes that you are using multiple virtual machines under Microsoft Virtual PC. In the optional projects for this lab, Projects 1.3 and 1.4, you will configure the second and third servers necessary to perform the optional projects in future lessons.

The instructor PC is preconfigured as a domain controller in the lucernepublishing.com domain for demonstration purposes; it is named INSTRUCTOR01.

 NOTE *In this lab you will see the characters zz. When you see these characters, substitute the two-digit number assigned to your computer.*

For ease of reference, record the static IP addresses of each server that you will be working with in this lab:

Writeable Domain Controller: (RWDCzz)

IP Address: ___.___.___.___

Subnet Mask: ___.___.___.___

Default Gateway: ___.___.___.___

Read-Only Domain Controller: (RODCzz)

IP Address: ___.___.___.___

Subnet Mask: ___.___.___.___

Default Gateway: ___.___.___.___

Server Core: (SCDCzz)

IP Address: ___.___.___.___

Subnet Mask: ___.___.___.___

Default Gateway: ___.___.___.___

SCENARIO

You are a network support specialist for Lucerne Publishing. Lucerne Publishing has implemented the lucernepublishing.com Active Directory forest as a single-domain environment. You are responsible for preparing several Windows Server 2008 servers to be deployed as domain controllers in remote offices. Because these servers were configured with only the default installation options, you have several tasks.

After completing this lab, you will be able to:

■ Explore the Windows Server 2008 interface to become familiar with its administration.

■ Modify basic settings on a Windows Server 2008 server.

■ Configure TCP/IP to prepare the Windows Server 2008 computer for promotion to domain controller status.

■ (Optional) Configure a Server Core computer.

Estimated lesson time: 100 minutes

Project 1.1	Modifying Basic Server Settings
Overview	You have just installed a new Windows Server 2008 computer using the default installation settings. You need to modify some basic settings on the server before you can configure it as a domain controller.
Outcomes	After completing this project, you will know how to: • Log on to a Windows Server 2008 computer. • Explore the Initial Configuration Tasks interface. • Modify basic settings on a Windows Server 2008 computer.
Completion time	10 minutes
Precautions	N/A

1.   Press Ctrl+Alt+Delete on the first Windows Server 2008 computer assigned to you and log on as the default administrator of the local computer. Your username is Administrator. The password is MSPress#1 or the password that your instructor or lab proctor has assigned to you. The Initial Configuration Tasks window will be displayed automatically, as shown in Figure 1-1.

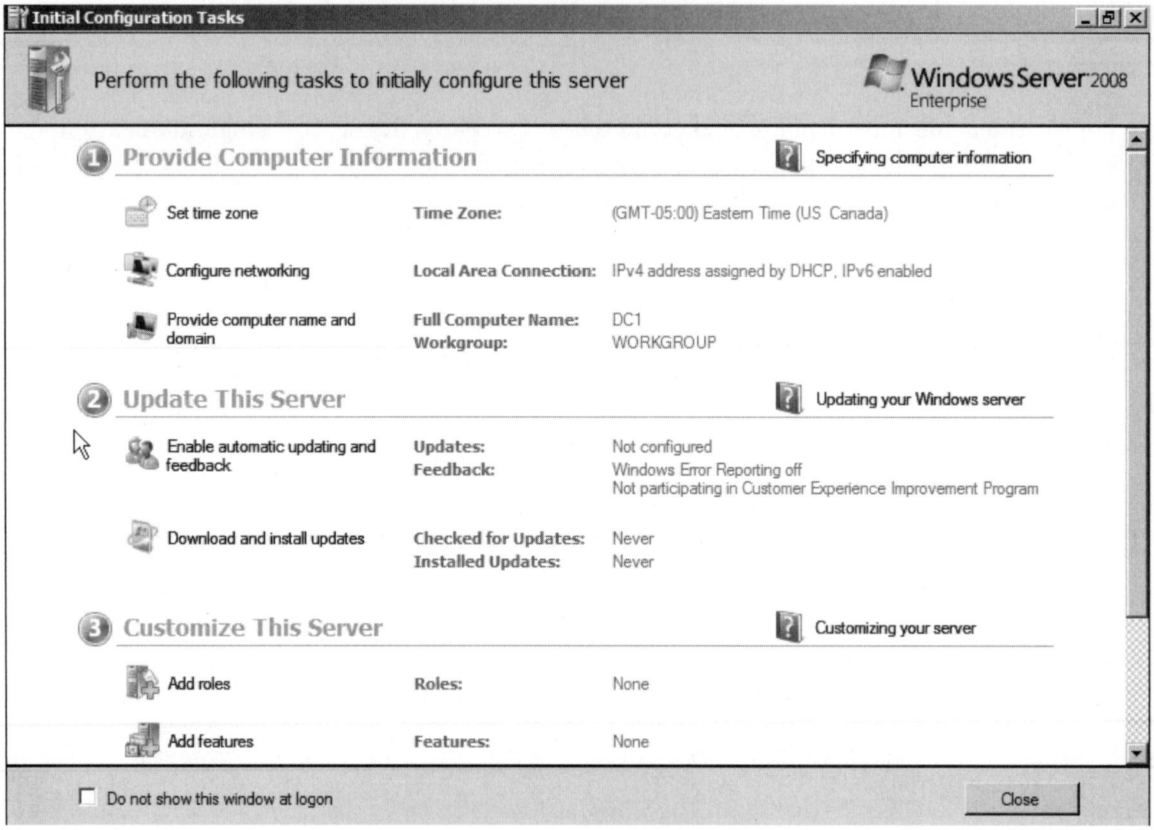

Figure 1-1
Initial Configuration Tasks window

2. Expand the Initial Configuration Tasks window to fill the screen, if necessary.

Question 1	*What are the three main tasks listed on the Initial Configuration Tasks window?*
Question 2	*What is the current time zone configured for this computer?*

3. Click Set Time Zone. The Date And Time window will be displayed.

4. Click Change Time Zone. The Time Zone Settings window will be displayed.

5. In the Time Zone dropdown box, select the appropriate time zone and click OK. You will return to the Date And Time window.

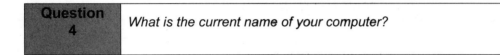

Question 3	Why does a shield icon appear next to the Change Date And Time button?

6. Click OK to return to the Initial Configuration Tasks window.

7. Click Enable Automatic Updating And Feedback. The Enable Windows Automated Updating And Feedback window is displayed.

8. Click Enable Windows Automatic Updating And Feedback (Recommended), and then click Close.

9. Click Provide Computer Name And Domain. The System Properties window will be displayed.

Question 4	What is the current name of your computer?

10. On the Computer Name tab, click Change. The Computer Name/Domain Changes window is displayed.

11. In the Computer Name text box, key **RWDCzz** for your computer name, where *zz* corresponds to the student number that your instructor or lab proctor has assigned to you. Click OK. A Computer Name/Domain Changes dialog box is displayed, informing you that you must restart your computer to apply these changes. Click OK to acknowledge this dialog box.

12. Click Close to close the System Properties window. You will be prompted to restart your computer to apply the name change. Click Restart Now. Your Windows Server 2008 computer will automatically restart.

Project 1.2	Configuring TCP/IP Settings
Overview	Your manager assigned to you the task of preparing a new Windows Server 2008 computer to function as a domain controller. To begin, you must configure this computer with static IP address settings.
Outcomes	After completing this project, you will know how to: • Configure network settings on a Windows Server 2008 computer.
Completion time	15 minutes
Precautions	The instructions presume that the lab environment has been configured using the 192.168.1.0/24 Class C address range, with addresses 192.168.1.100 through 192.168.1.130 reserved for assigning static IP addresses to student computers. If your lab environment uses a different IP addressing scheme, your instructor or lab proctor will provide the appropriate IP addressing values.

1. Press Ctrl+Alt+Delete on the Windows Server 2008 computer and log on as the default administrator of the local computer. Your username will be Administrator. The password will be MSPress#1 or the password that your instructor or lab proctor has assigned to you. The Initial Configuration Tasks window will be displayed automatically.

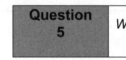

Question 5	*What name is assigned to your computer?*

2. Place a checkmark next to Do Not Show This Window At Logon. Click Close to close the Initial Configuration Tasks window. The Server Manager window is displayed automatically, as shown in Figure 1-2. Expand the Server Manager window to fill the screen, if necessary.

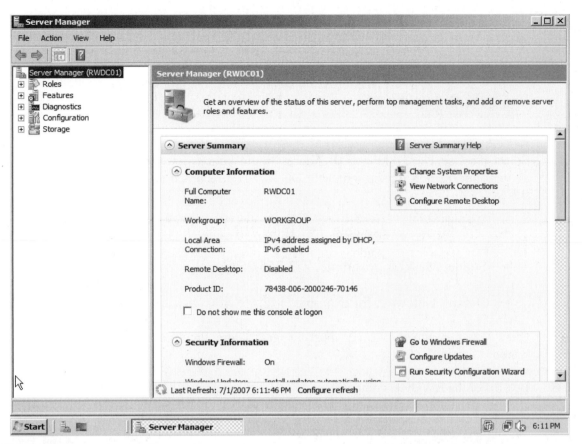

Figure 1-2
Server Manager window

3. Click View Network Connections. The Network Connections window is displayed.

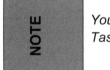
> *You can also configure network settings from the Initial Configuration Tasks screen.*

4. Right-click your network connection and select Properties. The network connection's Properties window will be displayed.

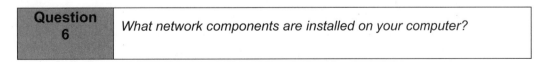
| Question 6 | *What network components are installed on your computer?* |

5.   Click Internet Protocol Version 4 (TCP/IPv4) and select Properties. The Internet Protocol Version 4 (TCP/IPv4) Properties window will be displayed.

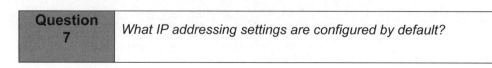

Question 7	*What IP addressing settings are configured by default?*

6.   Select the Use The Following IP Address radio button. Enter the following IP address information for the writeable DC that you recorded at the beginning of this lab.

- IP Address: for example, 192.168.1.101

- Subnet Mask: for example, 255.255.255.0

- Default Gateway: for example, 192.168.1.1

7.   Click OK two times to save your changes. Close the Network Connections window.

8.   Log off of the RWDC*zz* computer.

Project 1.3 (Optional) ·	Configuring a Second Windows Server 2008 Computer
Overview	Your manager assigned to you the task of preparing an additional Windows Server 2008 computer to function as a Read-Only Domain Controller in one of your branch offices. To begin, you must set up this computer with basic configuration information and static IP address settings.
Outcomes	After completing this project, you will know how to: • Log on to a Windows Server 2008 computer. • Explore the Initial Configuration Tasks interface. • Modify basic settings on a Windows Server 2008 computer. • Configure network settings on a Windows Server 2008 computer.
Completion time	25 minutes
Precautions	N/A

■ PART A: Configure Basic Settings on the Second Windows Server 2008 Computer

1. Press Ctrl+Alt+Delete on the second Windows Server 2008 computer assigned to you and log on as the default administrator of the local computer. Your username will be Administrator. The password will be MSPress#1 or the password that your instructor or lab proctor has assigned to you. The Initial Configuration Tasks window will be displayed automatically. Expand the Initial Configuration Tasks window to fill the full screen, if necessary.

2. Click Set Time Zone. The Date And Time window will be displayed.

3. Click Change Time Zone. The Time Zone Settings window will be displayed.

4. In the Time Zone dropdown box, select the appropriate time zone and click OK. You will return to the Date And Time window.

5. Click OK to return to the Initial Configuration Tasks window.

6. Click Enable Automatic Updating And Feedback. Click Enable Windows Automatic Updating And Feedback (Recommended), and then click Close.

7. Click Provide Computer Name And Domain. The System Properties window will be displayed.

Question 8	What is the current name of your computer?

8. On the Computer Name tab, click Change. The Computer Name/Domain Changes window will appear.

9. In the Computer name text box, enter **RODC**zz for your computer name, where zz corresponds to the student number that your instructor or lab proctor has assigned to you. Click OK. A Computer Name/Domain Changes dialog box will be displayed, informing you that you must restart your computer to apply these changes. Click OK to acknowledge this dialog box.

10. Click Close to close the System Properties window. You will be prompted to restart your computer to apply the name change. Click Restart Now. Your Windows Server 2008 computer will automatically restart.

■ PART B: Configure a Static IP Address on the Second Windows Server 2008 Computer

1. Press Ctrl+Alt+Delete on the RODCzz server and log on as the default administrator of the local computer. Your username will be Administrator. The password will be MSPress#1 or the password that your instructor or lab proctor has assigned to you. The Initial Configuration Tasks window will be displayed automatically.

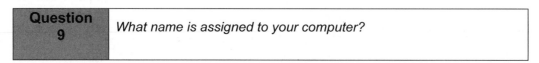

Question 9	What name is assigned to your computer?

2. Place a checkmark next to Do Not Show This Window At Logon. Click Close to close the Initial Configuration Tasks window. The Server Manager screen will be displayed automatically. Expand the Server Manager window to fit the full screen, if necessary.

3. Click View Network Connections. The Network Connections window will be displayed.

4. Right-click your network connection and select Properties. The network connection's Properties window will be displayed.

5. Click Internet Protocol Version 4 (TCP/IPv4) and select Properties. The Internet Protocol Version 4 (TCP/IPv4) Properties window will be displayed.

6. Select the Use The Following IP Address radio button. Enter the following IP address information for the Read-Only Domain Controller that you recorded at the beginning of this lab.

    • IP Address: for example, 192.168.1.101

    • Subnet Mask: for example, 255.255.255.0

    • Default Gateway: for example, 192.168.1.1

7. Click OK two times to save your changes. Close the Network Connections window.

8. Log off of the RODCzz server.

Project 1.4 (Optional)	Configuring a Windows Server 2008 Server Core Computer
Overview	Your manager assigned to you the task of preparing an additional Windows Server 2008 computer running Server Core to function as a domain controller in one of your branch offices. To begin, you must set up this third Windows Server 2008 computer with basic configuration information and static IP address settings. Because this server is running the Server Core installation option, you must perform most of the configuration from the command line.
Outcomes	After completing this project, you will know how to: • Log on to a Windows Server 2008 Server Core computer. • Modify basic settings on a Windows Server 2008 Server Core computer. • Configure network settings on a Windows Server 2008 Server Core computer. • Enable remote administration exceptions in the Windows Firewall of a Server Core computer.
Completion time	20 minutes
Precautions	N/A

■ PART A: Configure the Server Time Zone and Computer Name

1. Press Ctrl+Alt+Delete on the third Windows Server 2008 computer assigned to you and log on as the default administrator of the local computer. Your username will be Administrator. The password will be MSPress#1 or the password that your instructor or lab proctor has assigned to you. (If this is the first time that anyone has logged onto the Server Core computer, the initial password will be blank and you will be prompted to configure a new password that is not blank.)

Question 10	*What do you see when you log on to a Server Core computer?*

2. Key **timedate.cpl** at the command prompt and press Enter. The Date And Time window is displayed.

3. Click Change Time Zone. The Time Zone Settings window will be displayed.

4. In the Time Zone dropdown box, select the appropriate time zone and click OK. You will return to the Date And Time window. Click OK to return to the command prompt.

5. Key **hostname** and press Enter.

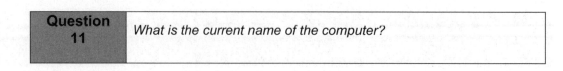

Question 11	What is the current name of the computer?

6. Key **netdom /?** and press Enter.

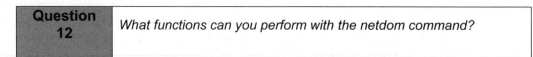

Question 12	What functions can you perform with the netdom command?

7. Key **netdom renamecomputer** *<Computername>* **/newname:SCDCzz**, substituting the name of the current computer for *<Computername>* and press Enter.

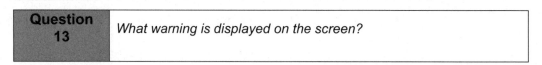

Question 13	What warning is displayed on the screen?

8. Key **y** and then press Enter.

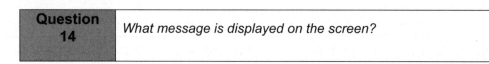

Question 14	What message is displayed on the screen?

9. Key **shutdown /r** and press Enter. A pop-up window informs you that Windows will shut down in less than a minute. Click Close and allow the computer to restart.

■ PART B: Configure a Static IP Address

1. Press Ctrl+Alt+Delete on the third Windows Server 2008 computer, and log on as the default administrator of the local computer. Your username will be Administrator. The password will be MSPress#1 or the password that your instructor or lab proctor has assigned to you.

2. Key **ipconfig /all** and press Enter.

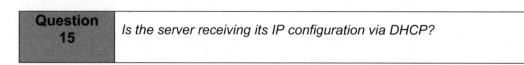

Question 15	Is the server receiving its IP configuration via DHCP?

3. Key **netsh** and then press Enter. Key **?** and press Enter.

Question 16	*What subcommands are available from the netsh menu?*

4. Key **interface** and then press Enter. Key **?** and press Enter.

Question 17	*What subcommands are available from the interface submenu?*

5. Key **ipv4** and then press Enter. Key **?** and press Enter.

Question 18	*What subcommands are available from the ipv4 menu?*

6. Key **set address name="Local Area Connection" source=static address=<*IP Address*> mask=<*Subnet Mask*> gateway=<*Default Gateway*> gwmetric=1**, substituting the appropriate values for the IP address, subnet mask and default gateway. Press Enter to assign this static IP configuration. Key **exit** to return to the command prompt.

7. Key **ipconfig /all** and press Enter.

Question 19	*Is the computer's IP address now statically assigned?*

■ PART C: Enable Remote Administration of the Server Core Computer

1. Press Ctrl+Alt+Delete on the third Windows Server 2008 computer and log on as the default administrator of the local computer. Your username will be Administrator. The password will be MSPress#1 or the password that your instructor or lab proctor has assigned to you.

2. Key **netsh advfirewall set allprofiles settings remotemanagement enable** to allow remote access to the server via the Computer Management MMC, the C$ shares, etc., and then press Enter.

3. Log off of the computer.

LAB REVIEW QUESTIONS

Completion time	15 minutes

1. In your own words, describe what you learned by completing this lab.

2. Open the Server Manager console on your Windows Server 2008 computer. What selections are available to you in the left pane?

3. Using the Windows Help option, describe any roles and features that are currently installed on this server.

4. Explain in your own words why it is a best practice to configure a domain controller with a static IP address, rather than allowing it to obtain an IP address using DHCP.

5. Explore the netsh command menus. Record three commands that you can issue from the command line using netsh and describe what each command does:

LAB CHALLENGE 1.1	VERIFYING ACTIVE DIRECTORY SRV RECORDS
Overview	Your manager just completed the installation of a domain controller in the lucernepublishing.com domain. You must verify that the SRV record for the domain controller was properly created in DNS.
Outcomes	After completing this project, you will know how to: • Verify the creation of SRV records for Active Directory domain controllers.
Completion time	15 minutes
Precautions	N/A

Verify that the classroom or lab domain SRV records have been created. Use the nslookup.exe utility to complete this challenge. Make and save a screen capture of your nslookup results. (Hint: Search the Microsoft Web site using the keyword "nslookup.exe.")

LAB 2
INSTALLING ACTIVE DIRECTORY DOMAIN SERVICES

This lab contains the following projects and activities:

Project 2.1	Installing the Active Directory Domain Services Role
Project 2.2	Installing a New Forest and Domain
Project 2.3	Verifying SRV Record Creation
Project 2.4	Creating User Accounts for Lab Use
Project 2.5	Installing a Child Domain
Project 2.6	Verifying Child Domain SRV Records
Project 2.7	Installing a Read-Only Domain Controller (Optional)
Project 2.8	Installing a Server Core Domain Controller (Optional)
Lab Review Questions	
Lab Challenge 2.1	Verifying That the Kerberos SRV Record Exists for the Child Domain

BEFORE YOU BEGIN

Lab 2 assumes that setup has been completed as specified in the setup document and that your computer has connectivity to other lab computers and the Internet. Lab 2 also assumes that you have completed the projects in the previous lab, including completing the Initial Configuration Tasks and configuring each server with a static IP address.

Lab 2 contains two optional projects to configure a Read-Only Domain Controller on a full installation of Windows Server 2008, as well as a domain controller that is running on Server Core. You can use multiple physical computers or you can use Microsoft Virtual PC or Virtual Server to install and run multiple servers on a single machine. This manual assumes you are using multiple virtual machines under Microsoft Virtual PC.

If you skip the optional projects for this lesson, you will be unable to complete future optional projects later in this manual.

In this lab you will see the characters xx, yy, and zz. When you see these characters, substitute the two-digit number assigned to your computer. These directions assume that you are working on computers configured in pairs, and that each computer has a number. One number is odd and the other number is even. For example, the first student pair will consist of RWDC01 as the first odd-numbered computer and RWDC02 as the first even-numbered computer, RODC01 and RODC02 as the second pair, and SCDC01 and SCDC02 as the third pair. When you see xx in this manual, substitute the unique number assigned to the odd-numbered computer in a pair. When you see yy, substitute the unique number assigned to the even-numbered computer in a pair. When you see zz, substitute the number assigned to the computer that you are currently working at, regardless of whether it is odd or even.

Lab 2 Dependencies

You must complete Lab 1, Project 1.2, for this lab to work properly.

For ease of reference, record the static IP addresses of each server that you will be working with in this lab:

Writeable Domain Controller:

Server Name: RWDC___ (Insert the *xx* number of the odd-numbered student.)

IP Address: ___.___.___.___

Subnet Mask: ___.___.___.___

Default Gateway: ___.___.___.___

Read-Only Domain Controller:

Server Name: RODC__ (Insert the *yy* number of the even-numbered student.)

IP Address: ___.___.___.___

Subnet Mask: ___.___.___.___

Default Gateway: ___.___.___.___

Server Core:

IP Address: ___.___.___.___

Subnet Mask: ___.___.___.___

Default Gateway: ___.___.___.___

SCENARIO

You are the network administrator of Tailspin Toys. You are assigned to install a new forest root for the company. After you complete the installation, you must verify that the installation was successful. Then, you must install a child domain in the new forest. During this lab, you will perform several tasks.

After completing this lab, you will be able to:

- Create an Active Directory forest and domain tree.

- Install a child domain and domain controller.

- Verify SRV records.

- Install a Read-Only Domain Controller (optional).

- Install a Server Core Domain Controller (optional).

- Automate the installation of Active Directory.

Estimated lesson time: 115 minutes

Project 2.1	Installing the Active Directory Domain Services Role
Overview	You have just installed a new Windows Server 2008 computer using the default installation settings. Now, you need to add the Active Directory Domain Services role before you can configure it as a domain controller.
Outcomes	After completing this project, you will know how to: • Add the Active Directory Domain Services role to a Windows Server 2008 computer using Server Manager.
Completion time	10 minutes
Precautions	Be sure that you have completed Project 1.2 in Lab 1 before beginning this project.

1. Press Ctrl+Alt+Delete on the RWDC*zz* computer. For example, if you are Student01, this will be the RWDC01 computer; if you are Student07, this will be the RWDC07 computer, and so on. Log on as the default administrator of the local computer. Your username will be Administrator. The password will be MSPress#1 or the password that your instructor or lab proctor has assigned to you. The Server Manager window will be displayed automatically. Expand the Server Manager window to fit the full screen, if necessary.

 | *What is the name of the computer you are working from?*

2. In the left pane of Server Manager, double-click Roles.

3. Click Add Role. Click Next to bypass the initial Welcome window. The Select Server Roles window is displayed.

4. Place a checkmark next to Active Directory Domain Services. Click Next. The Active Directory Domain Services window is displayed.

5. Read the introductory information about Active Directory Domain Services and click Next. The Confirm Installation Selections window is displayed.

6. Read the confirmation information to prepare for the installation. Click Install to install the Active Directory Domain Services role. The Installation Results window is displayed.

7. Read the information contained on this window and click Close.

Question 2	*What does this window indicate must be done next?*

8. Log out of the Windows Server 2008 computer or continue on to the next project.

Project 2.2	**Installing a New Forest and Domain**
Overview	Your manager has assigned you to install a new Active Directory environment. You must begin by installing the forest root domain controller in the forest root domain. In this project, you will install Active Directory on the RWDC*xx* computer in the lab. The new domain for each lab pair will be named domain*xx*.local, using the number of the odd-numbered student, (domain01, domain03, domain05, etc.). You will allow the Active Directory Installation Wizard to install and configure the Domain Name System (DNS) service automatically.
Outcomes	After completing this project, you will know how to: • Configure the forest root domain in a new Active Directory forest.
Completion time	20 minutes
Precautions	This project is to be completed only on the odd-numbered RWDC*xx* computers, such as RWDC01, RWDC03, RWDC05, RWDC07, and so on.

1. Press Ctrl+Alt+Delete on the odd-numbered RWDC*xx* computer and log on as the default administrator of the local computer. Your username will be Administrator. The password will be MSPress#1 or the password that your instructor or lab proctor has assigned to you. The Server Manager window will be displayed automatically. Expand the Server Manager window to fit the full screen, if necessary.

2. In the left pane of Server Manager, double-click Roles. In the right pane, you will see the number of roles that are installed on this server and the names of those roles.

Question 3	*What roles are currently installed?*
Question 4	*Why do you think this role has a red 'X' next to it?*

3. Click Active Directory Domain Services. The Active Directory Domain Services window is displayed.

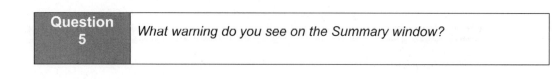

Question 5	What warning do you see on the Summary window?

4. Click Run The Active Directory Domain Services Installation Wizard (dcpromo.exe).

5. Place a checkmark next to Use Advanced Mode Installation and click Next. The Operating System Compatibility window is displayed.

6. Read the presented information and then click Next. The Choose A Deployment Configuration window is displayed.

7. Click the Create A New Domain In A New Forest radio button and click Next. The Name The Forest Root Domain window is displayed.

8. Key **domainxx.local** as the FQDN of the forest root domain. For example, if you are Student01, key domain01.local. Click Next to continue. The Domain NetBIOS Name is displayed.

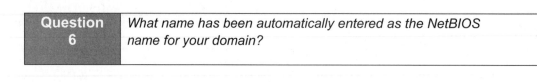

Question 6	What name has been automatically entered as the NetBIOS name for your domain?

9. Click Next to accept the default NetBIOS name. The Set Forest Functional Level window is displayed.

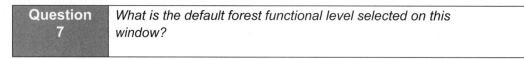

Question 7	What is the default forest functional level selected on this window?

10. Select Windows Server 2003 from the Forest Functional Level dropdown box and click Next. The Set Domain Functional Level window is displayed. Notice that the default option is now Windows Server 2003.

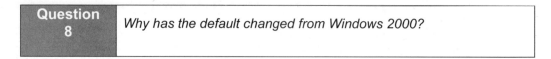

Question 8	Why has the default changed from Windows 2000?

11. Click Next to accept Windows Server 2003 as the domain functional level. The Additional Domain Controller Options window is displayed.

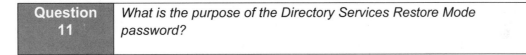

Question 9	Which options are selected by default? Which option is grayed out to indicate that it is mandatory? Why is this option mandatory?

12. Accept the default selections and click Next. One or more Active Directory Domain Services Installation Wizard warning windows are displayed sequentially.

13. Read each warning and click Yes to continue. The Location For Database, Log Files, And SYSVOL window is displayed.

Question 10	What are the default locations for the Active Directory Domain Services files?

14. Click Next to accept the default selections and continue. The Directory Services Restore Mode Administrator Password window is displayed.

15. Key **MSPress#1** or the password provided by your instructor or lab proctor in the Password and Confirm Password text boxes, and click Next to continue. The Summary window is displayed.

Question 11	What is the purpose of the Directory Services Restore Mode password?

16. Review your installation choices and click Next to continue. The Active Directory Domain Services Installation Wizard window is displayed, indicating that the Active Directory Domain Services service is being installed. Then, the Completing The Active Directory Domain Services Installation Wizard is displayed.

17. Click Finish. When prompted, click Restart Now to restart the newly configured domain controller.

Project 2.3	Verifying SRV Record Creation
Overview	You have just completed the installation of a domain controller. Your colleague asks you to verify the Lightweight Directory Access Protocol (LDAP) service locations (SRV) resource record for the domain controller.
Outcomes	After completing this project, you will know how to: • Use nslookup to verify DNS SRV records.
Completion time	5 minutes
Precautions	N/A

1. Press Ctrl+Alt+Delete on the RWDC*zz* computer (the odd-numbered student will log onto RWDC*xx* and the even-numbered student will log onto RWDC*yy*) and log on as the built-in Administrator of the forest root domain (on the RWDC*xx* computer) or as the default administrator of the local computer (on the RWDC*yy* computer). Your username will be Administrator. The password will be MSPress#1 or the password that your instructor or lab proctor has assigned to you.

Question 12	*If you are working on the RWDCxx computer, how has the login window changed now that you have promoted this computer to domain controller status?*

2. Open a command-prompt window.

3. Key **nslookup** in the command-prompt window. Press Enter.

NOTE	*If you see an error message that says "Can't find server name for that address," followed by the IP address of your server, this means that your DNS server does not have a reverse lookup zone configured. You can disregard this error for now. For more information on reverse lookup zones, as well as about the format of SRV records, refer to Lesson 12 or search the Microsoft TechNet Website.*

4. Key **set type=srv** and press Enter.

5. Key **_ldap._tcp.dc._msdcs.domain*xx*.local** and press Enter. If you are working on the RWDC*xx* computer, the LDAP SRV resource record for the domain controller of your domain is displayed, as shown in Figure 2-1. If you are working at the RWDC*yy* computer, an error message is displayed. The error message indicates that the lookup operation timed out or that the domain does not exist.

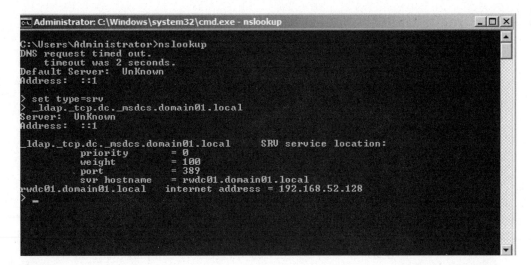

Figure 2-1
Message displayed

Question 13	*Why does the RWDCyy computer receive this error message?*

6. Key **exit** and press Enter.

7. Close the command-prompt window and log off of the Windows Server 2008 computer.

Project 2.4	Creating User Accounts for Lab Use
Overview	You have just completed the installation of a domain controller. Now, you will create dedicated user accounts for each student in your lab pair to prepare for subsequent projects in this lab.
Outcomes	After completing this project, you will know how to: • Create an Active Directory user account. • Add an Active Directory user account to an Active Directory group.
Completion time	10 minutes
Precautions	This project must be completed on the RWDC*xx* lab computer, which has been configured as a domain controller in the domain*xx*.local forest root domain. Students can work in turns, but these steps must be completed on the odd-numbered computer only.

■ PART A: Create a User Account for Each Student in the Lab Pair

1. Press Ctrl+Alt+Delete on the RWDC*xx* computer and log on as the built-in Administrator account of the forest root domain. Your username will be Administrator. The password will be MSPress#1 or the password that your instructor or lab proctor has assigned to you.

2. Click the Start button, click Administrative Tools, and then click Active Directory Users And Computers. Maximize the Active Directory Users And Computers window, if necessary.

3. Click the plus sign (+) next to domain*xx*.local. Click the Users container.

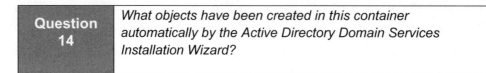

Question 14	What objects have been created in this container automatically by the Active Directory Domain Services Installation Wizard?

4. Right-click Users, select New, and then select User. The New Object–User window is displayed.

5. In the Full Name and User Logon Name fields, key **student*xx***. Notice that the User Logon Name (pre–Windows 2000) field was populated automatically.

Question 15	What is denoted by "@domainxx.local" in the dropdown box next to the User Logon Name field?

Question 16	What value do you see in the User Logon Name (pre–Windows 2000) field?

6. Click Next to continue. The New Object–User window is displayed.

7. In the Password and Confirm password fields, key **MSPress#1** or the password provided by your instructor or lab proctor as the password for student*xx*. Remove the checkmark next to User Must Change Password At Next Logon.

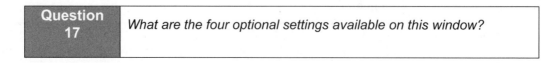

Question 17	What are the four optional settings available on this window?

8. Click the Next button. Review your selections, and then click Finish to create the student*xx* user account.

9. Repeat steps 4 through 8 to create a user account for student*yy*, the student on the RWDC*yy* computer.

10. Close the Active Directory Users And Computers console when you are finished or continue on to Part B.

■ PART B: Configure the Student Accounts with Administrative Access to the Forest Root Domain

1. Press Ctrl+Alt+Delete on the RWDC*xx* computer and log on as the built-in Administrator account of the forest root domain. Your username will be Administrator. The password will be MSPress#1 or the password that your instructor or lab proctor has assigned to you.

2. Click the Start button, click Administrative Tools, and then click Active Directory Users And Computers. Maximize the Active Directory Users And Computers window, if necessary.

3. Click the plus sign (+) next to domain*xx*.local. Click the Users container.

4. Right-click Enterprise Admins and select Properties.

Question 18	*What is the group scope and group type of the Enterprise Admins group? Can you change either of these settings?*

5. Click the Member tab.

Question 19	*What object(s) belong to the Enterprise Admins group by default?*

6. Click Add. The Select Users, Contacts, Computers, Or Groups window is displayed, as shown in Figure 2-2.

Figure 2-2
Select Users, Contacts, Computers, Or Groups window

7. Key **studentxx** and click OK.

8. Repeat steps 6 and 7 to add student*yy* to the Enterprise Admins group.

9. Click OK and close the Active Directory Users And Computers window.

10. Log off of the Windows Server 2008 domain controller.

Project 2.5	Installing a Child Domain
Overview	Your manager has assigned you to install a child domain for your company's existing Active Directory forest. In this project, you will configure Active Directory on the RWDC*yy* computers as a child domain named child*yy*. For example, if you are working at RWDC02, you will install a child domain named child02.domain01.local.
Outcomes	After completing this project, you will know how to: • Configure DNS settings on a Windows Server 2008 computer. • Configure a child domain in an existing Active Directory forest.
Completion time	20 minutes
Precautions	This project is to be completed only on the RWDC*yy* computers, such as RWDC02, RWDC04, RWDC06, RWDC08, and so on.

■ **PART A: Configure the Even-Numbered RWDC*yy* Computer to Perform DNS Resolution for the domain*xx*.local Domain**

1. Press Ctrl+Alt+Delete on the even-numbered RWDC*yy* computer and log on as the default administrator of the local computer. Your username will be Administrator. The password will be MSPress#1 or the password that your instructor or lab proctor has assigned to you. The Server Manager window is displayed automatically. Expand the Server Manager window to fit the full screen, if necessary.

2. Click View Network Connections. The Network Connections window is displayed.

3. Right-click your network connection and select Properties. The network connection's Properties window is displayed.

4. Click Internet Protocol Version 4 (TCP/IPv4) and select Properties. The Internet Protocol Version 4 (TCP/IPv4) Properties window is displayed.

5. Select the Use The Following DNS Server Addresses radio button. In the Preferred DNS Server text box, enter the IP address information for the writeable domain controller that is configured as the domain controller for domain*xx*.local, as configured in Project 2.2.

6. Click OK two times to save your changes. Close the Network Connections window.

7. Log off of the RWDC*yy* computer or continue to Part B.

■ **PART B: Configure the RWDC*yy* Computer as the First Domain Controller in the child*yy*.domain*xx*.local Child Domain in the domain*xx*.local Active Directory Forest**

1. Press Ctrl+Alt+Delete on the even-numbered RWDC*yy* computer and log on as the default administrator of the local computer. Your username will be Administrator. The password will be MSPress#1 or the password that your instructor or lab proctor has assigned to you. The Server Manager window is displayed automatically. Expand the Server Manager window to fit the full screen, if necessary.

2. In the left pane of Server Manager, double-click Roles. In the right pane, you will see the number of roles that are installed on this server and the names of those roles.

3. Click Active Directory Domain Services. The Active Directory Domain Services window is displayed.

4. Click Run The Active Directory Domain Services Installation Wizard (dcpromo.exe). Place a checkmark next to Use Advanced Mode Installation and click Next. The Operating System Compatibility window is displayed. Read the presented information and then click Next. The Choose A Deployment Configuration window is displayed.

5. Click the Existing Forest radio button, and then select Create A New Domain In An Existing Forest.

Question 20	*If you are creating a new domain tree instead of a child domain, what would you select on this window?*

6. Click Next. The Network Credentials window is displayed.

7. In the Type The Name Of Any Domain In The Forest Where You Plan To Install This Domain Controller text box, key **domain*xx*.local**, the name of the forest root domain.

8. Click Set to specify an alternate set of credentials to create the child domain. A Windows Security dialog box will be displayed.

Question 21	*Why can't you use the Administrator account on RWDCyy?*

9.   Key **student***yy* and the password for this account, and then click OK to close the dialog box.

10.   Click **Next**. The Name The New Domain window is displayed.

11.   In the FQDN Of The Parent Domain text box, key **domain***xx***.local**. In the Single-label DNS Name Of The Child Domain text box, key **child***yy*. For example, the child domain for domain01.local would have a single-label DNS name of child02.

Question 22	What is the FQDN of the new child domain?

12.   Click Next. The Domain NetBIOS Name window is displayed.

Question 23	What is the default NetBIOS name of the child domain?

13.   Click Next. The Set Domain Functional Level window is displayed.

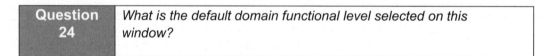

Question 24	What is the default domain functional level selected on this window?

14.   Click Next. The Select A Site window is displayed.

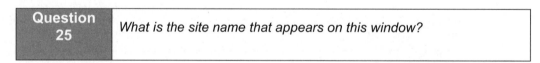

Question 25	What is the site name that appears on this window?

15.   Click Next. The Additional Domain Controller Options window is displayed.

Question 26	Which options are selected by default?

16.   Place a checkmark next to Global Catalog and DNS Server and click Next. An Active Directory Domain Services Installation Wizard warning window is displayed. Read the warning and click Yes to continue. The Source Domain Controller window is displayed.

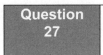 Question 27	*What is the default value selected on this window?*

17. Click Next. The Location for Database, Log Files, And SYSVOL window is displayed.

18. Click Next to accept the default values on this window. The Directory Services Restore Mode Administrator Password window is displayed.

19. Key **MSPress#1** in the Password and Confirm Password text boxes, and then click Next to continue. The Summary window is displayed.

20. Review your installation choices and click Next to continue. The Active Directory Domain Services Installation Wizard window is displayed, indicating that the Active Directory Domain Services service is being installed. The Completing The Active Directory Domain Services Installation Wizard is displayed.

21. Click Finish. When prompted, click Restart Now to restart the domain controller for the newly configured child domain.

■ PART C: Creating an Administrative Account in the Child Domain

1. Press Ctrl+Alt+Delete on the RWDC*yy* computer and log on as the built-in Administrator account of the forest root domain. Your username will be Administrator. The password will be MSPress#1 or the password that your instructor or lab proctor has assigned to you.

2. Click the Start button, click Administrative Tools, and then click Active Directory Users And Computers. Maximize the Active Directory Users And Computers window, if necessary.

3. Click the plus sign (+) next to child*yy*.domain*xx*.local. Click the Users container.

Question 28	*What objects have been created in this container automatically by the Active Directory Domain Services Installation Wizard?*

4. Right-click Users, select New, and then select User. The New Object–User window is displayed.

5. In the Full Name and User Logon Name fields, key **child*yy*student*yy***. Notice that the User Logon Name (pre–Windows 2000) field was populated automatically.

Question 29	What is denoted by '@childyy.domainxx.local' in the dropdown box next to the User Logon Name field?
Question 30	What value do you see in the User Logon Name (pre–Windows 2000) field?

6. Click Next to continue. The New Object–User window is displayed.

7. In the Password and Confirm password fields, key **MSPress#1** as the password for student*yy*. Remove the checkmark next to User Must Change Password At Next Logon.

8. Review your selections and then click Finish to create the student*yy* user account.

9. Click the plus sign (+) next to domain*xx*.local. Click the Users container.

10. Right-click Domain Admins and select Properties.

Question 31	What is the group scope and group type of the Domain Admins group? Can you change either of these settings?

11. Click the Member tab.

Question 32	What object(s) belong to the Domain Admins group by default?

12. Click Add. The Select Users, Contact, Computers, Or Groups window is displayed.

13. The Enter The Object Names To Select (Examples) window is displayed. Key **child*yy*student*yy*** and click OK.

Project 2.6	Verifying Child Domain SRV Records
Overview	You have just completed the installation of a child domain. Your colleague asks you to verify that the Lightweight Directory Access Protocol (LDAP) service locations (SRV) resource record was created on the parent domain's DNS server.
Outcomes	After completing this project, you will know how to: • Use nslookup to verify DNS SRV records.
Completion time	5 minutes
Precautions	For the student on the RWDC*xx* computer, complete Part A, "Verifying LDAP records for the Child Domain Using the DNS Console." For the student at the RWDC*yy* computer, complete Part B, "Verifying the LDAP Record for the Child Domain Using nslookup."

■ PART A: Verifying LDAP Records for the Child Domain Using the DNS Console

1. Press Ctrl+Alt+Delete on the RWDC*yy* computer and log on as the administrative account that was created in Project 2.4. Your username will be student*xx*. The password will be MSPress#1 or the password that your instructor or lab proctor has assigned to you.

2. Click the Start button, click Administrative Tools, and then click DNS Management.

3. Click the plus sign (+) next to the server name. Click Forward Lookup Zones, click domain*xx*.local, click child*yy*.domain*xx*.local, click _msdcs, and then click dc.

4. Click _tcp in the left pane. In the right pane, double-click _ldap.

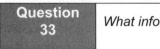 *What information is included in this entry?*

5. Close the DNS Management console.

6. Log off of the Windows Server 2008 computer.

■ PART B: Verifying LDAP Records for the Child Domain Using nslookup

1. Press Ctrl+Alt+Delete on the RWDC*yy* computer and log on as the administrative account that was created in Project 2.5. Your username will be student*yy*. The password will be MSPress#1 or the password that your instructor or lab proctor has assigned to you.

2. Open a command-prompt window.

3. Key **nslookup** and press Enter.

4. Key **set type=srv** and press Enter.

5. Key **_ldap._tcp.dc._msdcs.child*yy*.domain*xx*.local** and press Enter. A summary output is displayed, showing the LDAP SRV resource record for domain controllers within the child domain.

6. Key **exit** and press Enter.

7. Close the command-prompt window.

8. Log off of the Windows Server 2008 computer.

Project 2.7	Installing a Read-Only Domain Controller (Optional)
Overview	You have just completed the installation of the domain*xx*.local forest root domain and the child*yy*.domain*xx*.local child domain. Your organization supports a number of remote branch offices that do not have full-time IT staff in place, so your manager has tasked you with configuring Read-Only Domain Controllers to provide authentication for these offices.
Outcomes	After completing this project, you will know how to: • Install and configure a Read-Only Domain Controller. • Configure the Password Replication Policy for a Read-Only Domain Controller. • Designate a local administrator for a Read-Only Domain Controller.
Completion time	45 minutes
Precautions	This optional project assumes that you have completed Project 1.3 in Lab 1. If you are using virtualization software such as Virtual PC, running multiple virtual machines simultaneously may impact your computer's performance.

■ PART A: Create a Local Administrator for the Read-Only Domain Controller in the Forest Root Domain

> **NOTE** *This portion of the lab is to be completed on the RWDCxx computer, which is configured as the domain controller for the domainxx.local forest root domain. The even-numbered student can follow along with these steps or skip ahead to Part D.*

1. Press Ctrl+Alt+Delete on the RWDC*xx* computer and log on as the administrative account that was created in Project 2.4. Your username will be student*xx*. The password will be MSPress#1 or the password that your instructor or lab proctor has assigned to you.

2. Click the Start button, click Administrative Tools, and then click Active Directory Users and Computers. Maximize the Active Directory Users And Computers window, if necessary.

3. Click the plus sign (+) next to domain*xx*.local. Click the Users container. Right-click Users, select New, and then select User. The New Object–User window is displayed.

4. In the Full Name and User Logon Name fields, key **RODCadmin***xx*. Notice that the User Logon Name (pre–Windows 2000): field was populated automatically with the same value.

5. Click Next to continue. The New Object–User window is displayed.

6. In the Password and Confirm password fields, key **MSPress#1**. Remove the checkmark next to User Must Change Password At Next Logon.

7. Click the Next button. Review your selections, and then click Finish to create the RODCadmin*xx* user account. Notice that this user is not a member of any administrative group, such as Domain Admins or Enterprise Admins.

■ PART B: Create a Local Administrator for the Read-Only Domain Controller in the Child Domain

> *This part of the project is to be completed on the RWDCyy computer, which is configured as the domain controller for the childyy.domainxx.local forest root domain.*

1. Press Ctrl+Alt+Delete on the RWDC*yy* computer and log on as the administrative account for the child domain that was created in Project 2.6. Your username will be student*yy*. The password will be MSPress#1 or the password that your instructor or lab proctor has assigned to you.

2. Click the Start button, click Administrative Tools, and then click Active Directory Users And Computers. Maximize the Active Directory Users And Computers window, if necessary.

3. Click the plus sign (+) next to child*yy*.domain*xx*.local. Click the Users container. Right-click Users, select New, and then select User. The New Object–User window is displayed.

4. In the Full Name and User Logon Name fields, key **RODCadmin*yy***. Notice that the User Logon Name (pre–Windows 2000) field was populated automatically with the same value.

5. Click Next to continue. The New Object–User window is displayed.

6. In the Password and Confirm password fields, key **MSPress#1** or the password provided by your instructor or lab proctor. Remove the checkmark next to User Must Change Password At Next Logon.

7. Review your selections, and then click Finish to create the RODCadmin*yy* user account. Notice that this user is not a member of any administrative group, such as Domain Admins or Enterprise Admins.

■ PART C: Configure a Read-Only Domain Controller in the Forest Root Domain

<table>
<tr>
<td>NOTE</td>
<td>Parts C and D are to be completed on the RODCxx computer, which will be configured as an RODC in the domainxx.local forest root domain. The even-numbered student can follow along or skip ahead to Parts E and F.</td>
</tr>
</table>

1. Press Ctrl+Alt+Delete on the RODC*xx* computer and log on as the default administrator of the local computer. Your username will be Administrator. The password will be MSPress#1 or the password that your instructor or lab proctor has assigned to you. The Server Manager window will be displayed automatically. Expand the Server Manager window to fit the full screen, if necessary.

<table>
<tr>
<td>Question
34</td>
<td>What is the name of the computer you are using?</td>
</tr>
</table>

2. Click View Network Connections. The Network Connections window will be displayed.

3. Right-click your network connection and select Properties. The network connection's Properties window will be displayed.

4. Click Internet Protocol Version 4 (TCP/IPv4) and select Properties. The Internet Protocol Version 4 (TCP/IPv4) Properties window will be displayed.

5. Select the Use The Following DNS Server Addresses radio button. In the Preferred DNS Server text box, enter the IP address information for the writeable DC that is configured as the domain controller for domain*xx*.local, as configured in Project 2.2.

6. Click OK two times to save your changes. Close the Network Connections window to return to the Server Manager console.

7. In the left pane of Server Manager, double-click Roles.

8. Click Add Role. Click Next to bypass the initial Welcome window. The Select Server Roles window is displayed.

9. Place a checkmark next to Active Directory Domain Services. Click Next. The Active Directory Domain Services window is displayed.

10. Read the introductory information to Active Directory Domain Services and click Next. The Confirm Installation Selections window is displayed.

11. Read the confirmation information to prepare for the installation. Click Install to install the Active Directory Domain Services role. The Installation Results window is displayed.

12. Click Close This Wizard And Launch The Active Directory Domain Services Installation Wizard (dcpromo.exe). The Welcome To The Active Directory Domain Services Installation Wizard window is displayed.

13. Place a checkmark next to Use Advanced Mode Installation and click Next. The Operating System Compatibility window is displayed. Read the presented information and click Next. The Choose A Deployment Configuration window is displayed.

14. Click the Existing Forest radio button, and then click Add A Domain Controller To An Existing Domain and click Next. The Network Credentials window will be displayed.

15. In the Type The Name Of Any Domain In The Forest Where You Plan To Install This Domain Controller text box, key **domainxx.local**.

16. Click Set to specify an alternate set of credentials to add the new domain controller. A Windows Security dialog box will be displayed.

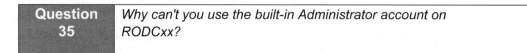

Question 35	Why can't you use the built-in Administrator account on RODCxx?

17. Key **studentxx** and the password for this account, then click OK. The Select A Domain window is displayed.

18. Select the domainxx.local domain and click Next. The Select A Site window is displayed.

19. Accept the default value and click Next. The Additional Domain Controller Options window is displayed.

20. Place a checkmark next to Read-only Domain Controller (RODC) and click Next. An Active Directory Services Installation Wizard window is displayed. Read the warning and click Yes to continue. The Specify The Password Replication Policy window is displayed.

21. Confirm the list of users, groups, and computers that are configured with an Allow or Deny entry in the Password Replication Policy, and click Next to continue. The Delegation Of RODC Installation And Administration window is displayed.

22. Click Set to specify a local administrator for the Read-Only Domain Controller that does not have administrative permissions within Active Directory. The Select User Or Group window is displayed.

23. Key **RODCadmin***xx* and click OK. Click Next. The Location For Database, Log Files, And SYSVOL window is displayed.

24. Accept the default selections and click Next to continue. The Directory Services Restore Mode Administrator Password window is displayed.

25. Key **MSPress#1** or the password provided by your instructor or lab proctor in the Password and Confirm Password text boxes and click Next to continue. The Summary window is displayed.

26. Review your installation choices and click Next to continue. The Active Directory Domain Services Installation Wizard window is displayed, indicating that the Active Directory Domain Services service is being installed. The Completing The Active Directory Domain Services Installation Wizard is displayed.

27. Click Finish. When prompted, click Restart Now to restart the newly configured domain controller.

■ PART D: Confirm Local Administrator Functionality on the Forest Root Read-Only Domain Controller

This part of the project is to be completed on the odd-numbered RODCxx computer, which has been configured as a Read-Only Domain Controller in the domainxx.local forest root domain. This exercise will confirm that the delegated administrator that you created in Part A does not have elevated privileges in the domainxx.local domain.

1. Press Ctrl+Alt+Delete on the RODC*xx* computer and log on as the delegated administrator created in Part A. Your username will be rodcadmin*xx*. The password will be MSPress#1 or the password that your instructor or lab proctor has assigned to you.

2. Click the Start button, click Administrative Tools, and then click Event Viewer. When you receive a UAC prompt, click Continue.

3. Click Windows Logs and then click Security.

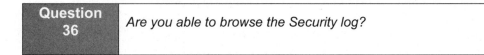
Question 36 | *Are you able to browse the Security log?*

4. Close the Event Viewer.

5. Click the Start button, click Administrative Tools, and then click Active Directory Users And Computers. When you receive a UAC prompt, click Continue.

6. Browse as needed to select domain*xx*.local and then click Users. Right-click Administrator and click Reset Password. Enter a new password in the New Password and Confirm Password dialog boxes, and then click OK.

Question 37	Are you able to change the password for the Active Directory Administrator account?

7. Click Cancel. Close the Active Directory Users And Computers console.

8. Log off of the RODC*yy* computer.

■ PART E: Configure a Read-Only Domain Controller in the Child Domain

NOTE	This part of the project is to be completed on the RODC*yy* computer, which will be configured as a Read-Only Domain Controller in the child*yy*.domain*xx*.local child domain.

1. Press Ctrl+Alt+Delete on the RODC*yy* computer and log on as the default administrator of the local computer. Your username will be Administrator. The password will be MSPress#1 or the password that your instructor or lab proctor has assigned to you. The Server Manager window will be displayed automatically. Expand the Server Manager window to fit the full screen, if necessary.

Question 38	What is the name of the computer you are working from?

2. Click View Network Connections. The Network Connections window will be displayed. Right-click your network connection and select Properties. The network connection's Properties window will be displayed.

3. Click Internet Protocol Version 4 (TCP/IPv4) and select Properties. The Internet Protocol Version 4 (TCP/IPv4) Properties window will be displayed.

4. Select the Use The Following DNS Server Addresses radio button. In the Preferred DNS Server text box, enter the IP address information for the writeable DC that is configured as the domain controller for child*yy*.domain*xx*.local, as configured in Project 2.5.

5. Click OK two times to save your changes. Close the Network Connections window to return to the Server Manager console.

6. In the left pane of Server Manager, double-click Roles.

7. Click Add Role. Click Next to bypass the initial Welcome window. The Select Server Roles window is displayed.

8. Place a checkmark next to Active Directory Domain Services. Click Next. The Active Directory Domain Services window is displayed.

9. Read the introductory information to Active Directory Domain Services and click Next. The Confirm Installation Selections window is displayed.

10. Read the confirmation information to prepare for the installation. Click Install to install the Active Directory Domain Services role. The Installation Results window is displayed.

11. Click Close This Wizard And Launch The Active Directory Domain Services Installation Wizard (dcpromo.exe). The Welcome To The Active Directory Domain Services Installation Wizard window is displayed.

12. Place a checkmark next to Use Advanced Mode Installation and click Next. The Operating System Compatibility window is displayed. Read the presented information and click Next. The Choose A Deployment Configuration window is displayed.

13. Click the Existing Forest radio button, click Add A Domain Controller To An Existing Domain, and then click Next. The Network Credentials window will be displayed.

14. In the Type The Name Of Any Domain In The Forest Where You Plan To Install This Domain Controller text box, key **child*yy*.domain*xx*.local**.

15. Click Set to specify an alternate set of credentials to add the new domain controller. A Windows Security dialog box will be displayed.

Question 39	*Why can't you use the built-in Administrator account on RODCxx?*

16. Key **domain*xx*\student*yy*** and the password for this account, and then click OK. The Select A Domain window is displayed.

17. Select the child*yy*.domain*xx*.local domain and click Next. The Select A Site window is displayed.

18. Accept the default value and click Next. The Additional Domain Controller Options window is displayed.

19. Place a checkmark next to Read-only Domain Controller (RODC) and click Next. An Active Directory Services Installation Wizard window is displayed. Read the warning and click Yes to continue. The Specify The Password Replication Policy window is displayed.

20. Confirm the list of users, groups, and computers that are configured with an Allow or Deny entry in the Password Replication Policy, and click Next to continue. The Delegation Of RODC Installation And Administration window is displayed.

21. Click Set to specify a local administrator for the Read-Only Domain Controller that does not have administrative permissions within Active Directory. The Select User Or Group window is displayed.

22. Key **childyy.domainxx.local\RODCadminyy** and click OK. Click Next. The Location For Database, Log Files, And SYSVOL window is displayed.

23. Accept the default selections and click Next to continue. The Directory Services Restore Mode Administrator Password window is displayed.

24. Key **MSPress#1** in the Password and Confirm Password text boxes and click Next to continue. The Summary window is displayed.

25. Review your installation choices and click Next to continue. The Active Directory Domain Services Installation Wizard window is displayed, indicating that the Active Directory Domain Services service is being installed. The Completing The Active Directory Domain Services Installation Wizard is displayed.

26. Click Finish. When prompted, click Restart Now to restart the newly configured domain controller.

■ PART F: Confirm Local Administrator Functionality on the Child Domain Read-Only Domain Controller

> NOTE
>
> *This part of the project is to be completed on the RODCyy computer, which has been configured as a Read-Only Domain Controller in the childyy.domainxx.local child domain.*

1. Press Ctrl+Alt+Delete on the RODC*yy* computer and log on as the delegated administrator created in Part B. Your username will be rodcadmin*yy*. The password will be MSPress#1 or the password that your instructor or lab proctor has assigned to you.

2. Click the Start button, click Administrative Tools, and then click Event Viewer. When you receive a UAC prompt, click Continue.

3.   Click Windows Logs and then click Security.

Question 40	Are you able to browse the Security log?

4.   Close the Event Viewer.

5.   Click the Start button, click Administrative Tools, and then click Active Directory Users And Computers. When you receive a UAC prompt, click Continue.

6.   Browse as needed to select child*xx*.domain*xx*.local and then click Users. Right-click Administrator and click Reset Password. Key a new password in the New Password and Confirm Password dialog boxes and then click OK.

Question 41	Are you able to change the password for the Active Directory Administrator account?

7.   Click Cancel, and then close the Active Directory Users And Computers console.

8.   Log off of the RODC*yy* computer.

Project 2.8	Installing a Server Core Domain Controller (Optional)
Overview	You have just completed the installation of the domain*xx*.local forest root domain and the child*yy*.domain*xx*.local. Your manager has tasked you with configuring domain controllers running on Windows Server 2008 Server Core.
Outcomes	After completing this project, you will know how to: • Configure DNS name resolution on a Server Core computer. • Create an unattend.txt file to perform an automated dcpromo.
Completion time	30 minutes
Precautions	This optional project assumes that you have completed Project 1.4 in Lab 1. Part A of this project is to be performed on the odd-numbered Server Core computer, which is named SCDC*xx*. Part B of this project is to be performed on the even-numbered Server Core computer, which is named SCDC*yy*.

■ PART A: Configure a Server Core Domain Controller in the Forest Root Domain

1. Press Ctrl+Alt+Delete on the odd-numbered SCDC*xx* computer and log on as the built-in local Administrator account. Your username will be Administrator. The password will be MSPress#1 or the password that your instructor or lab proctor has assigned to you.

2. In the command-prompt window, key **netsh interface ipv4 set dnsserver name="Local Area Connection" source=static address=<*IP Address of RWDCxx*> index=1** and then press Enter. Key **ipconfig /all**.

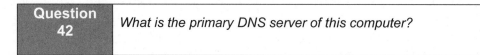

Question 42	What is the primary DNS server of this computer?

3. Key **notepad** and then press Enter.

4. Enter the following text into the Notepad window to create an unattended configuration file for the dcpromo process.

[DCInstall]

; Replica DC promotion

ReplicaOrNewDomain=Replica

ReplicaDomainDNSName=domain*xx*.local

SiteName=Default-First-Site-Name

InstallDNS=Yes

ConfirmGc=Yes

UserDomain=domain*xx*.local

UserName=domain*xx*.local\student*xx*

Password=MSPress#1

DatabasePath="C:\Windows\NTDS"

LogPath="C:\Windows\NTDS"

SYSVOLPath="C:\Windows\SYSVOL"

SafeModeAdminPassword=MSPress#1

5. Save the file as **c:\unattend.txt** and close Notepad.

6. At the command prompt, key **dcpromo /unattend:c:\unattend.txt** and then press Enter. The computer will reboot automatically when the dcpromo process has completed.

7. Press Ctrl+Alt+Delete on the SCDC*xx* computer and log on as the administrative account that was created in Project 2.4. Your username will be student*xx*. The password will be MSPress#1 or the password that your instructor or lab proctor has assigned to you.

8. From the command-prompt window, key **notepad c:\unattend.txt** and press Enter.

Question 43	*What values are listed next to the Password= and SafeModeAdminPassword= entries?*

9. Log off of the SCDC*xx* computer.

■ PART B: Configure a Server Core Domain Controller in the Child Domain

1. Press Ctrl+Alt+Delete on the SCDC*yy* computer and log on as the built-in local Administrator account. Your username will be Administrator. The password will be MSPress#1 or the password that your instructor or lab proctor has assigned to you.

2. In the command-prompt window, key **netsh interface ipv4 set dns name="Local Area Connection" source=static address=<IP Address of RWDC*yy*>** and then press Enter. Key **ipconfig /all**.

Question 44	*What is the primary DNS server of this computer?*

3. Key **notepad** and then press Enter.

4. Enter the following text into the Notepad window.

[DCInstall]

; Replica DC promotion

ReplicaOrNewDomain=Replica

ReplicaDomainDNSName=child*yy*.domain*xx*.local

SiteName=Default-First-Site-Name

InstallDNS=Yes

ConfirmGc=Yes

UserDomain=child*yy*.domain*xx*.local

UserName=child*yy*.domain*xx*.local\student*yy*

Password=MSPress#1

DatabasePath="C:\Windows\NTDS"

LogPath="C:\Windows\NTDS"

SYSVOLPath="C:\Windows\SYSVOL"

SafeModeAdminPassword=MSPress#1

5. Save the file as **c:\unattend.txt** and close Notepad.

6. At the command prompt, key **dcpromo /unattend:c:\unattend.txt** and then press Enter. The computer will reboot automatically when the dcpromo process has completed.

7. Press Ctrl+Alt+Delete on the SCDC*yy* computer and log on as the administrative account that was created in Project 2.6. Your username will be student*xx*. The password will be MSPress#1 or the password that your instructor or lab proctor has assigned to you.

8. From the command-prompt window, key **notepad c:\unattend.txt** and press Enter.

Question 45	*What values are listed next to the Password= and SafeModeAdminPassword= entries?*

9. Log off of the SCDC*yy* computer.

LAB REVIEW QUESTIONS

Completion time	15 minutes

1. In your own words, describe what you learned by completing this lab.

2. When a child domain is installed and the parent domain is hosting an Active Directory–integrated DNS server that allows dynamic updates, are the SRV resource records of the child domain added automatically during Active Directory installation?

3. How is a child domain represented in the Domain Name System (DNS) console?

4. Which domain controller establishes the name of the forest?

5. Whether you are installing a child domain or the first domain in a forest, what are some common parameters you define for the Active Directory installation process?

LAB CHALLENGE 2.1	VERIFYING THAT THE KERBEROS SRV RECORD EXISTS FOR THE CHILD DOMAIN
Overview	The security administrator for your company wants to know if the Kerberos Key Distribution Center (KDC) record is available for your domain.
Outcomes	After completing this project, you will know how to: • Verify the creation of the Kerberos SRV records for an Active Directory child domain.
Completion time	5 minutes
Precautions	N/A

Each domain controller registers several service locator (SRV) resource records. One of these records identifies the Kerberos KDC, which is also the domain controller. Use nslookup to verify that this record exists for the child domain. Use the Technet Website if you wish to learn more about SRV records for Active Directory, as well as the use of the nslookup command.

LAB 3
WORKING WITH ACTIVE DIRECTORY SITES

This lab contains the following projects and activities:

Project 3.1   Replication Management

Project 3.2   Preparing Your Infrastructure

Project 3.3   Configuring a Site

Project 3.4   Configuring a New Subnet

Project 3.5   Moving Computers and Creating Site Links

Lab Review Questions

Lab Challenge 3.1   Configuring Preferred Bridgehead Servers for Sites

Lab Challenge 3.2   Making the Even-Numbered Computer a Global Catalog Server

Post-lab Cleanup

BEFORE YOU BEGIN

Lab 3 assumes that setup has been completed as specified in the setup document, and that your computer has connectivity to other lab computers and the Internet. Lab 3 also assumes that you have completed the nonoptional projects in the previous labs. Specifically, Lab 3 assumes the following:

- The even-numbered computer (RWDC*yy*) must be configured to use the odd-numbered computer (RWDC*xx*) as its preferred DNS server, as explained in Lab 1, Project 1.4.
- Active Directory is installed on the odd-numbered computer (RWDC*xx*), as described in Lab 2, Project 2.1 and Project 2.2.
- Active Directory is installed on the even-numbered computer (RWDC*yy*), as described in Lab 2, Project 2.5.

NOTE

In this lab, you will see the characters xx, yy, and zz. These directions assume that students are working in pairs, and that each student has a number. One number is odd and the other number is even. For example, the first student pair will consist of RWDC01 as the first odd-numbered computer and RWDC02 as the first even-numbered computer, RWDC03 and RWDC04 as the second student pair, and RWDC05 and RWDC06 as the third student pair. When you see "xx" in this manual, substitute the unique number assigned to the odd-numbered computer in a pair. When you see "yy", substitute the unique number assigned to the even-numbered computer in a pair. **When you see "zz", substitute the number assigned to the computer that you are currently working at, regardless of whether it is odd or even.**

If you have completed all exercises in the previous lessons, including the optional exercises, the lab environment for Student01 and Student02 will resemble the topology shown in Figure 3-1.

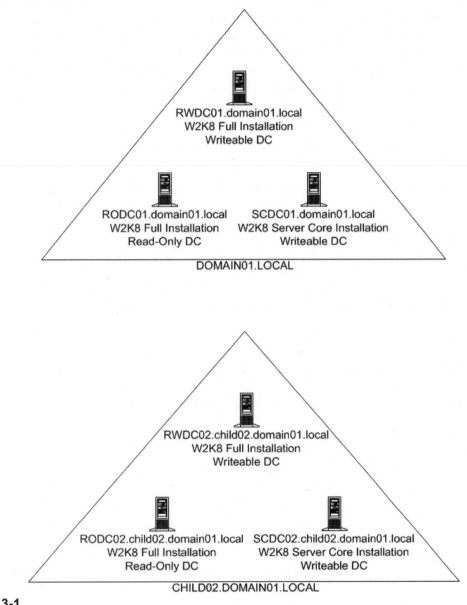

Figure 3-1
Lab environment

SCENARIO

You are a network administrator for the contoso.com domain. Contoso.com contains two domain controllers running Microsoft Windows Server 2008, Enterprise Edition. However, you are preparing to install several more domain controllers in the near future as your company expands. These new locations will be separated from the contoso.com headquarters by slow wide area network (WAN) links. You must prepare your existing structure to support multiple sites. Before you do this, you must verify your existing site structure. When the remote locations are added, you must add a site for each location. Finally, you must investigate the configuration of additional global catalog servers for the new remote locations. During this lab, you will perform several tasks.

After completing this lab, you will be able to:

- Use Active Directory Sites and Services and repadmin to manage Active Directory sites.

- View a replication topology.

- Create Active Directory sites.

- Configure bridgehead servers between sites.

- Configure a global catalog server.

Estimated lesson time: 145 minutes

Project 3.1	Replication Management
Overview	You want to verify that the site's domain controllers are replicating information properly. You have reviewed the replication error messages in the Event Viewer Directory Service log and identified some errors that you are anxious to resolve. First, you plan to force replication. Then, you plan to create a manual connection object. Finally, you will use repadmin to troubleshoot any further problems.
Outcomes	After completing this project, you will know how to: • Force Active Directory replication. • Manage Active Directory connection objects. • Identify a global catalog server. • Use repadmin to troubleshoot Active Directory replication.
Completion time	60 minutes
Precautions	On the odd-numbered computer (RWDC*xx*), be sure to log on using the Administrator account in the domain*xx*.local domain. On the even-numbered computer (RWDC*yy*), log on using the Administrator account in the child*yy*.domain*xx*.local domain.

■ PART A: Forcing Replication

1. Press Ctrl+Alt+Delete on the RWDC*zz* computer and log on with administrative credentials to the domain for this domain controller; for odd-numbered computers the domain will be domain*xx*.local and for even-numbered computers the domain will be child*yy*.domain*xx*.local. Your username will be Administrator. The password will be MSPress#1 or the password that your instructor or lab proctor has assigned to you. Close the Server Manager window when it is displayed automatically.

2. To open the Active Directory Sites And Services MMC snap-in, click Start, click Administrative Tools, and then click Active Directory Sites And Services.

3. In the left pane, expand the Sites folder.

Question 1	*What is the name of the site that was created by default when you installed the Active Directory Domain Services role?*

4. Expand the Click the Default-First-Site-Name site. Click the Servers folder.

Question 2	*What servers are listed within this folder?*

5. Expand the icon for the server that you are using. In the left pane, click NTDS Settings.

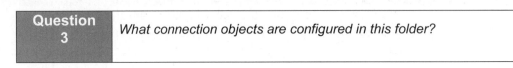

Question 3	What connection objects are configured in this folder?

6. In the right pane, select one of the replication connections that has been configured for your server. Right-click the connection and then click Replicate Now. A Replicate Now message box is displayed, as shown in Figure 3-2, indicating that Active Directory has replicated the connection.

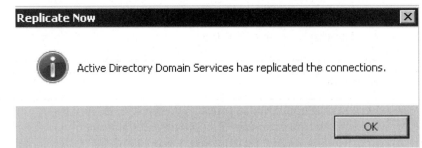

Figure 3-2
Replicate Now dialog box

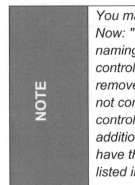

You may see the following error message when you select Replicate Now: "The following error occurred during the attempt to synchronize naming context Configuration from domain controller RWDCxx to domain controller RWDCyy. The naming context is in the process of being removed or is not replicated from the specified server. The operation will not continue." If you receive this error, wait a few minutes for the domain controllers to synchronize and then try again to force a replication. In addition, if you do not complete the optional labs in Lab 2, you will not have the RODC01 or SCDC01. Therefore, you will only have one server listed in the NTDS settings.

7. Click OK. Close the Active Directory Sites And Services console.

■ PART B: Managing Connection Objects

Suppose that your attempt to force replication did not work. In this case, you could check the Event Viewer's Directory Service log to learn what occurred. Let's say that you decide there may be a problem with the connections objects and decide to create one manually as a temporary troubleshooting measure. (It is not a best practice to configure manual connection objects for everyday replication, because they can become stale or out-of-date. This project is designed to illustrate creating a manual connection object for troubleshooting purposes only.)

1. Open the Active Directory Sites and Services console. In the left console pane, expand the Sites folder, and then expand the Default-First-Site-Name.

2. Expand the Sites folder, and then expand the computer name of the server that you are using. In the left console pane, click NTDS Settings.

3. Right-click NTDS Settings, and then click New Active Directory Domain Services Connection. The Find Domain Controllers dialog box is displayed.

4. Select the name of your partner's computer. For example, if you are using RWDC01, select RWDC02 from the list of computer names displayed in the Search Results window pane; if you are using RWDC02, select RWDC01 from the list of computer names displayed in the Search Results window pane. Click OK. An Active Directory message box is displayed, indicating that there is already a connection and asking you if you want to create another connection.

5. Click Yes. A New Object-Connection dialog box is displayed, as shown in Figure 3-3.

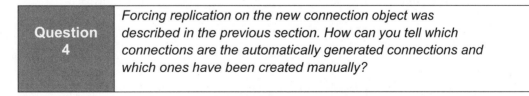

Figure 3-3
New Object-Connection dialog box

6. To accept the default settings, click OK. The new connection is created. Two connections should be displayed: the automatically generated connection and the manually generated connection.

Question 4	Forcing replication on the new connection object was described in the previous section. How can you tell which connections are the automatically generated connections and which ones have been created manually?

7. In the right pane, right-click the manually created connection and click Delete. An Active Directory message box is displayed.

8. Click Yes to confirm that you want to delete the connection object. The object is deleted.

■ PART C: Identifying the Global Catalog

While performing your replication checks, you learn that certain users are unable to log on to the network. You begin to wonder if the global catalog server is functional. You need to verify which server is functioning as the global catalog server.

1. In the Active Directory Sites And Services console's left pane, right-click NTDS Settings and then click Properties. The NTDS Settings Properties dialog box is displayed.

2. On the General tab, you can see that the Global Catalog checkbox is selected. Click Cancel.

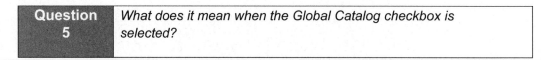

Question 5	What does it mean when the Global Catalog checkbox is selected?

3. Close the Active Directory Sites And Services console.

■ PART D: Using repadmin

You decide to force replication with repadmin this time. You also want to verify your replication partner connections.

1. Log in as Domainxx\Studentyy account for this to work.

2. Open a command-prompt window.

3. In the command-prompt window on the odd-numbered computer, key **repadmin /syncall childyy.domainxx.local**. In the command-prompt window on the even-numbered computer, key **repadmin /syncall domainxx.local**.

4. Read all of the repadmin command output. Confirm that the repadmin output includes an indication that "The following replication completed successfully." All domain controllers are now synchronized, as shown in Figure 3-4.

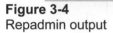

```
Administrator: C:\Windows\system32\cmd.exe                    _ □ X
C:\>repadmin /syncall child02.domain01.local
CALLBACK MESSAGE: The following replication is in progress:
    From: af6fa6b9-3006-4663-92e4-31f2fdd81d23._msdcs.domain01.local
    To  : 7c813b60-0ea4-463a-b447-8992cde3799e._msdcs.domain01.local
CALLBACK MESSAGE: The following replication completed successfully:
    From: af6fa6b9-3006-4663-92e4-31f2fdd81d23._msdcs.domain01.local
    To  : 7c813b60-0ea4-463a-b447-8992cde3799e._msdcs.domain01.local
CALLBACK MESSAGE: SyncAll Finished.
SyncAll terminated with no errors.


C:\>_
```

Figure 3-4
Repadmin output

5. On the odd-numbered computer, key **repadmin /showrepl childyy.domainxx.local**. On the even-numbered computer, key **repadmin /showrepl domainxx.local**.

Question 6	Who are your inbound neighbors?

6. Key **cls** and press Enter to clear the window.

7. On the odd-numbered computer, key **repadmin /showconn childyy.domainxx.local**. On the even-numbered computer, key **repadmin /showconn domainxx.local**.

Question 7	How many connections were found?

8. Close the command-prompt window.

Project 3.2	Preparing Your Infrastructure
Overview	You want to configure your existing network to support a new site so that you can run some tests to see how a custom application will perform. However, you are unable to locate a router or additional network cards. You decide that you can create a logical Internet Protocol (IP) network inside your physical local area network (LAN) for your tests. You need to prepare two servers for this test.
Outcomes	After completing this project, you will know how to: • Modify the TCP/IP configuration of a Windows Server 2008 computer.
Completion time	5 minutes
Precautions	Some of the steps in this project should only be performed on one computer in each pair. You will be informed which computer, odd or even, to use in the first step of each portion of this project.

■ PART A: Preparing the Odd-Numbered Computer for Site-Configuration Testing

1. Press Ctrl+Alt+Delete on the odd-numbered RWDCxx computer and log on as the default administrator of the domain*xx*.local domain. Your username will be Administrator. The password will be MSPress#1 or the password that your instructor or lab proctor has assigned to you. The Server Manager window is displayed automatically. Expand the Server Manager window to fit the full screen, if necessary.

2. Click View Network Connections. The Network Connections window is displayed.

3. Right-click your network connection and select Properties. The network connection's Properties window is displayed.

4. Click Internet Protocol Version 4 (TCP/IPv4) and select Properties. The Internet Protocol Version 4 (TCP/IPv4) Properties window is displayed.

5. Click Advanced. The Advanced TCP/IP Settings window is displayed.

6. On the IP Settings tab, click Add. The TCP/IP Address dialog box is displayed.

7. Enter the following additional IP address for this server:

    •   Key the IP address **192.168.x.x**. For example, RWDC05 would be configured as 192.168.5.5.

    •   Key the subnet mask **255.255.255.0**.

8. Click Add, and then click OK three times to save your settings.

■ PART B: Preparing the Even-Numbered Computer for Site-Configuration Testing

1. Press Ctrl+Alt+Delete on the RWDCyy computer and log on as the default administrator of the local computer. Your username will be Administrator. The password will be MSPress#1 or the password that your instructor or lab proctor has assigned to you. The Server Manager window is displayed automatically. Expand the Server Manager window to fit the full screen, if necessary.

2. Click View Network Connections. The Network Connections window is displayed.

3. Right-click your network connection and select Properties. The network connection's Properties window is displayed.

4. Click Internet Protocol Version 4 (TCP/IPv4) and select Properties. The Internet Protocol Version 4 (TCP/IPv4) Properties window is displayed.

5. Click Advanced. The Advanced TCP/IP Settings window is displayed.

6. On the IP Settings tab, click Add. The TCP/IP Address dialog box is displayed.

7. Enter the following additional IP address for this server:

    *   Key the IP address **192.168.y.y**. For example, RWDC06 would be configured as 192.168.6.6.

    *   Key the subnet mask **255.255.255.0**.

8. Click Add, and then click OK three times to save your settings. Figure 3-5 shows how the result of Project 3.2 might look for the Student01 and Student02 computer pair. (Note that your configuration may differ depending on the network configuration of your lab environment; see your instructor or proctor for guidance.)

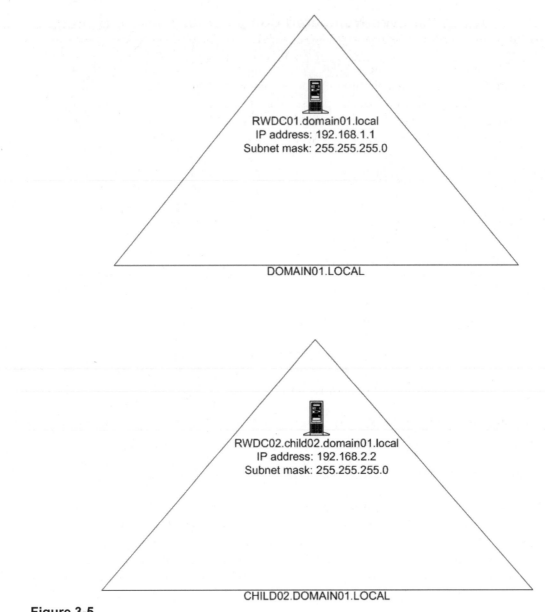

Figure 3-5
Configuration

Project 3.3	Configuring a Site
Overview	You decide to create the Main and Branch sites. Furthermore, you want to rename the Default-First-Site-Name to HQ.
Outcomes	After completing this project, you will know how to: • Create a new site. • Rename an existing site.
Completion time	5 minutes
Precautions	N/A

■ PART A: Creating a Site for the Odd-Numbered Computer

1. On the odd-numbered RWDC*xx* computer, open the Active Directory Sites And Services console.

2. In the left pane, right-click Sites and then click New Site. The New Object-Site dialog box is displayed.

3. In the Name text box, key **MainSite**. Click DEFAULTIPSITELINK and then click OK. A message box is displayed, indicating that you must complete additional steps to configure the site.

4. Click OK.

■ PART B: Creating a Site for the Even-Numbered Computer and Renaming the Default-First-Site-Name Site

1. Log onto the even-numbered RWDCyy computer using the Domainxx\Studentyy account in the domainxx.local domain, which is a member of the Enterprise Admins group in the forest root domain. On the even-numbered computer, open the Active Directory Sites And Services console. If you receive an error message indicating that the naming information cannot be located, wait a few minutes to ensure that the two domain controllers have had time to replicate and then try opening the console again.

2. In the left pane, right-click Sites and then click New Site. The New Object-Site dialog box is displayed.

3. In the Name text box, key **BranchSite**. Click DEFAULTIPSITELINK and then click OK. A message box is displayed, indicating that you must complete additional steps to configure the site.

4. Click OK.

5. In the left pane, right-click Default-First-Site-Name and then click Rename. Key **HQ** as the new name for Default-First-Site-Name and then press Enter. Your final site configuration should resemble the one shown in Figure 3-6.

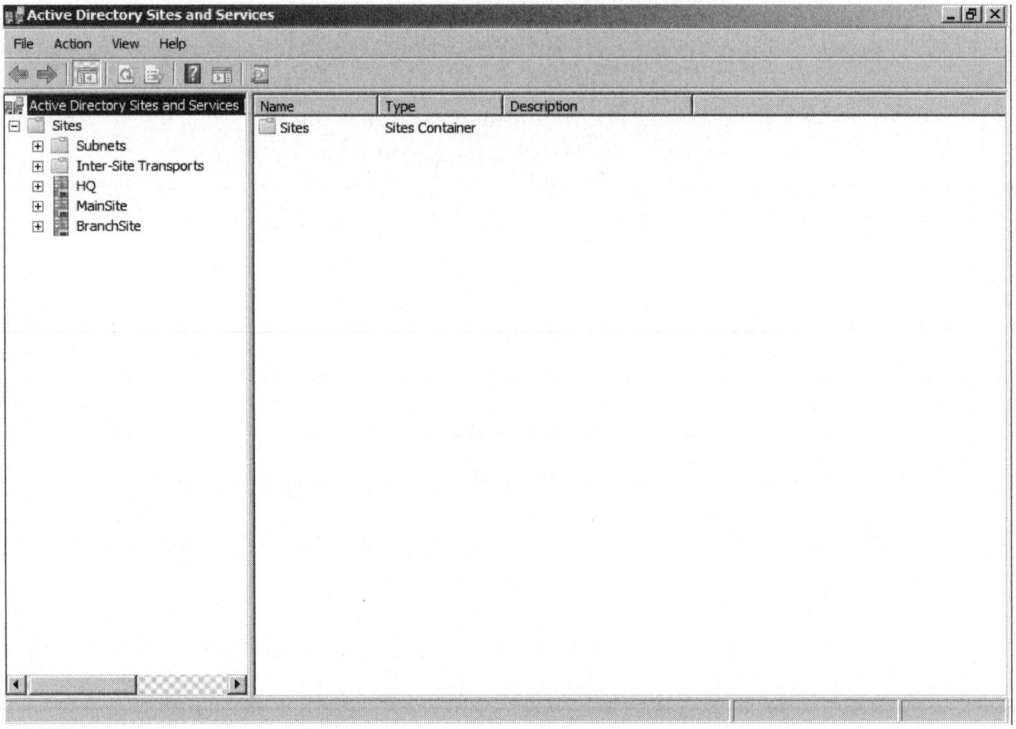

Figure 3-6
Final site configuration

Project 3.4	Configuring a New Subnet
Overview	To simulate inter-site Active Directory replication, you decide to create two new subnets for use in the two sites that you created in Project 3.3.
Outcomes	After completing this project, you will know how to: • Create an Active Directory subnet object.
Completion time	5 minutes
Precautions	Some of the steps in this project should only be performed on one computer in each pair. You will be informed which computer, odd or even, to use in the first step of each portion of this project.

■ PART A: Create a Subnet Object for the Odd-Numbered Computer

1. On the odd-numbered computer, open the Active Directory Sites And Services console.

2. In the left pane, right-click Subnets and then click New Subnet. The New Object-Subnet dialog box is displayed.

3. Key **192.168.x.0/24** in the Prefix text box; for example, on the RWDC01 computer, key 192.168.1.0/24. In the Site Name portion of the dialog box, click MainSite, as shown in Figure 3-7, and click OK.

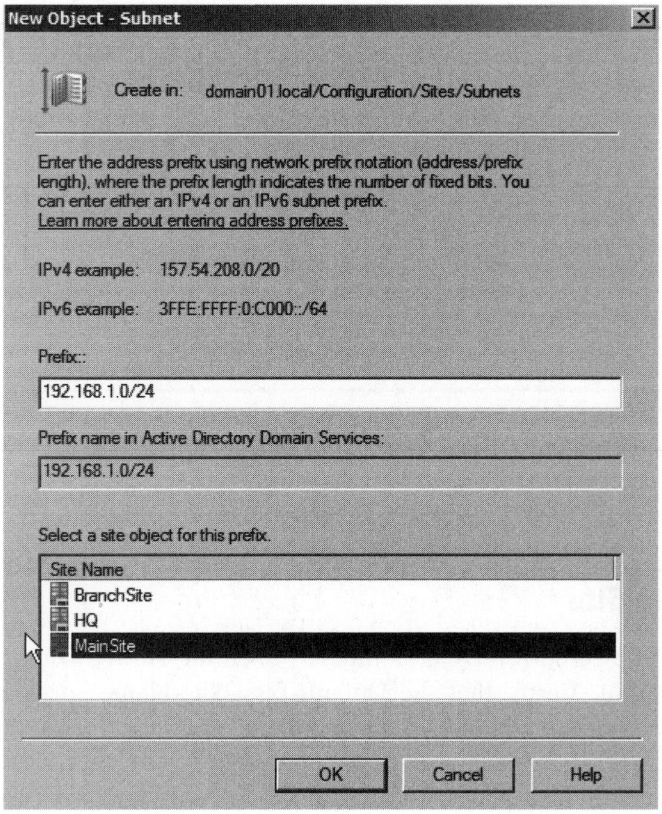

Figure 3-7
Object–Subnet dialog box

■ PART B: Create a Subnet Object for the Even-Numbered Computer

1. Log on to the RWDCyy computer using the Domainxx\Studentyy account in the domainxx.local domain, which is a member of the Enterprise Admins group in the forest root domain. On the even-numbered computer, open the Active Directory Sites And Services console.

2. Right-click Subnets, and then click New Subnet. The New Object–Subnet dialog box is displayed.

3. Key **192.168.y.0/24** in the Prefix text box; for example, on the RWDC02 computer, key 192.168.2.0/24. In the Site Name portion of the dialog box, click BranchSite, and then click OK.

Project 3.5	Moving Computers and Creating Site Links
Overview	Now that you have created site and subnet objects, you want to move your computer accounts into their respective sites and configure site links between the sites.
Outcomes	After completing this project, you will know how to: • Move a computer from one site to another. • Create and configure a site link object.
Completion time	15 minutes
Precautions	Some of the steps in this project should only be performed on one computer in each pair. You will be informed which computer, odd or even, to use in the first step of each portion of this project.

■ PART A: Moving the Odd-Numbered and Even-Numbered Computers to the Appropriate Site

1. On the odd-numbered RWDC*xx* computer, open the Active Directory Sites And Services console. Verify that the Default-First-Site-Name site was renamed to HQ. If you do not see this on the odd-numbered computer, force replication with the even-numbered computer and refresh the view. If a replication error is displayed, wait a few minutes and try again.

2. In the left pane, expand the HQ site and then expand the Servers folder.

3. Right-click RWDCxx, and then click Move. The Move Server dialog box is displayed.

4. Click MainSite and then click OK.

5. In the left pane, expand MainSite and then expand the Servers object below MainSite. You should see the odd-numbered computer object.

6. Try to force replicataion using the connection object of the odd-numbered computer. You should see a message indicating that these servers are in different sites. Click OK.

7. Right-click RWDCyy, and then click Move. The Move Server dialog box is displayed.

8. Click BranchSite and then click OK.

9. In the left pane, expand BranchSite and then expand the Servers folder. You should see the even-numbered computer object.

10. Try to force replication using the connection object of the even-numbered computer. You should see a message indicating that these servers are in different sites. Click OK. Your site configuration should resemble the site shown in Figure 3-8.

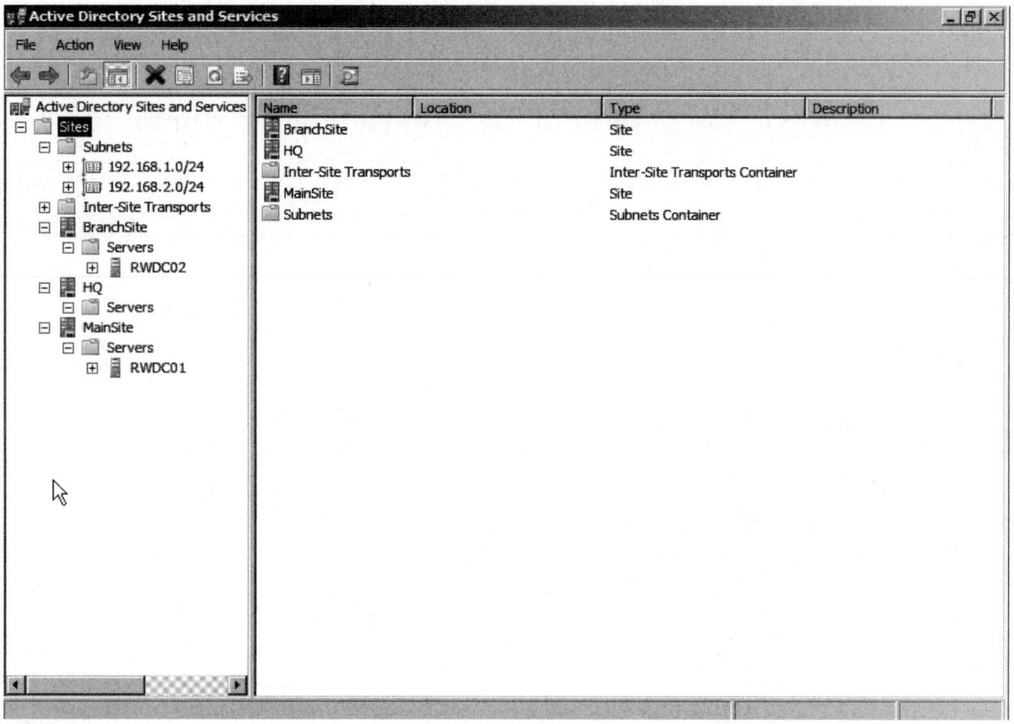

Figure 3-8
Site configuration

■ PART B: Creating a Site Link Object from the Even-Numbered Computer

For replication to take place between RWDC*xx* and RWDC*yy* in separate sites, you must create a site link object between these sites.

1. Log on to the even-numbered RWDC*yy* computer using the Domainxx\Studentyy account in the domainxx.local domain, which is a member of the Enterprise Admins group in the forest root domain. On the even-numbered computer, open the Active Directory Sites And Services console.

2. In the left pane, expand the Inter-Site Transports folder. Right-click IP and click New Site Link. The New Object-Site Link dialog box is displayed.

3. In the Name text box, key **EvenLink**. In the Sites Not In This Site Link box, click MainSite and then click Add.

4. In the Sites Not in This Site Link box, click BranchSite and then click Add. Click OK to save your changes.

5. Click the IP object under Inter-Site Transports. The EvenLink site link should be visible in the right pane.

6. Right-click EvenLink and click Properties. The Evenlink Properties dialog box is displayed.

7. Change the value in the Replicate Every box to 15 minutes, and then click OK.

■ PART C: Creating a Site Link from the Odd-Numbered Computer

In a production environment you would only create a single site link object between two sites. To allow both students to familiarize themselves with the process, however, in this project you will create two site link objects.

1. On the odd-numbered computer, open the Active Directory Sites And Services console.

2. In the left pane, expand the Inter-Site Transports folder. Right-click IP and then click New Site Link. The New Object-Site Link dialog box is displayed.

3. In the Name text box, key **OddLink**. In the Sites Not In This Site Link box, click MainSite and then click Add.

4. In the Sites Not In This Site Link box, click BranchSite and then click Add. Click OK to save your changes.

5. Click the IP object under Inter-Site Transports. The OddLink site link should be displayed in the right pane.

6. Right-click OddLink and click Properties. The Oddlink Properties dialog box is displayed.

7. Change the value in the Replicate Every box to 15 minutes, and then click OK.

■ PART D: Verifying Replications

1. Wait approximately 15 minutes for replication to complete. Return to the odd-numbered or even-numbered computer. Refresh the Active Directory Sites And Services console by pressing the F5 key or clicking the Refresh button on the toolbar.

2. Click Inter-Site Transports and then click IP. You should see both site link objects added as a site link. This provides verification that your computers are replicating with each other.

3. Complete the Lab Challenges. If you do not complete the Lab Challenges, you must perform the Lab Cleanup before you can move on to Lab 4.

LAB REVIEW QUESTIONS

Completion time	15 minutes

1. In your own words, describe what you learned by completing this lab.

2. Which default administrative group has the necessary privileges to create and monitor sites?

3. In a multidomain environment, what is the main difference between the partitions on a domain controller that is also a global catalog server, versus other domain controllers that are not configured as global catalog servers?

4. What major tasks are required to create an Active Directory site?

LAB CHALLENGE 3.1	CONFIGURING PREFERRED BRIDGEHEAD SERVERS FOR SITES
Overview	You noticed that the Knowledge Consistency Checker (KCC) is not selecting the server that you want Active Directory to use as the bridgehead server in each site. You decide to configure a preferred bridgehead server for your site.
Outcomes	After completing this project, you will know how to: • Configure a preferred bridgehead server.
Completion time	10 minutes
Precautions	If you do not complete the Lab Challenges, you must still perform the Lab Cleanup before you can move on to Lab 4.

Configure the odd-numbered computer as the preferred bridgehead server for the MainSite. Configure the even-numbered computer as the preferred bridgehead server for the BranchSite.

LAB CHALLENGE 3.2	MAKING THE EVEN-NUMBERED COMPUTER A GLOBAL CATALOG SERVER
Overview	You decide to make the computer in the BranchSite a global catalog server.
Outcomes	After completing this project, you will know how to: • Configure a global catalog server.
Completion time	20 minutes
Precautions	If you do not complete the Lab Challenges, you must still perform the Lab Cleanup before you can move on to Lab 4.

Confirm that the even-numbered RWDC*yy* server is configured as a global catalog server for the domain*xx*.local forest.

POST-LAB CLEANUP	
Overview	Use the techniques that you learned in this lab to complete the following steps from the odd-numbered computer, RWDC*xx*. These cleanup steps are required to reset the lab configuration to perform exercises in the following Labs.
Outcomes	N/A
Completion time	10 minutes
Precautions	Complete these steps only on the odd-numbered computer in each lab pair, except where indicated.

1. Press Ctrl+Alt+Delete on the RWDCxx computer and log on with administrative credentials to the domain*xx*.local domain. Your username will be Administrator. The password will be MSPress#1 or the password that your instructor or lab proctor has assigned to you.

2. Close the Server Manager window when it is displayed automatically.

3. Move the odd-numbered computer and the even-numbered computer into the HQ site.

4. Rename the HQ site to Default-First-Site-Name.

5. Clear the Global Catalog checkbox on the even-numbered computer's NTDS Settings Properties dialog box.

6. Delete the two sites created in this lab. To delete a site in the Active Directory Sites And Services console, right-click the site object that you want to remove and then click Delete. Confirm this action by clicking Yes on each of the two warning message boxes that are displayed.

7. Delete the two subnets created in this lab. To delete a subnet in the Active Directory Sites And Services console, expand the Subnets object, right-click the subnet object that you wish to remove, and then click Delete. Confirm this action by clicking Yes on the warning message that is displayed.

8. Delete the two site links created in this lab. To delete a site link object in the Active Directory Sites And Services console, expand the Inter-Site Transports object and then select the IP object. In the right pane, right-click the site link object that you want to remove and then click Delete. Confirm this action by clicking Yes on the warning message that is displayed.

9. Remove the additional IP address configured for the odd-numbered computer.

10. After the odd-numbered server has finished rebooting, remove the additional IP address configured for the even-numbered computer.

LAB 4
GLOBAL CATALOG AND FLEXIBLE SINGLE MASTER OPERATIONS (FSMO) ROLES

This lab contains the following projects and activities:

Project 4.1   The Global Catalog and the Windows Server 2008 Domain Functional Level

Project 4.2   Enabling Universal Group Membership Caching

Project 4.3   Working with Flexible Single Master Operations Roles

Lab Review Questions

Lab Challenge 4.1   Using the DNS Console to Verify Global Catalog Records on the DNS Server

Lab Challenge 4.2   Verifying FSMO Role Holders with DCDIAG

Lab Challenge 4.3   Determining Whether an Attribute Is Replicated in the Global Catalog

BEFORE YOU BEGIN

Lab 4 assumes that setup has been completed as specified in the setup document and that your computer has connectivity to other lab computers and the Internet. Lab 4 also assumes that you have completed the nonoptional exercises in the previous labs. Specifically, Lab 4 assumes the following:

- The even-numbered computer (RWDC*yy*) must be configured to use the odd-numbered computer (RWDC*xx*) as its preferred DNS server, as explained in Lab 1, Project 1.4.
- Active Directory is installed on the odd-numbered computer (RWDC*xx*), as described in Lab 2, Project 2.1 and Project 2.2.
- Active Directory is installed on the even-numbered computer (RWDC*yy*), as described in Lab 2, Project 2.5.

> **NOTE**
>
> *In this lab, you will see the characters xx, yy, and zz. These directions assume that students are working in pairs, and that each student has a number. One number is odd and the other number is even. For example, the first student pair will consist of RWDC01 as the first odd-numbered computer and RWDC02 as the first even-numbered computer, RWDC03 and RWDC04 as the second student pair, and RWDC05 and RWDC06 as the third student pair. When you see "xx" in this manual, substitute the unique number assigned to the odd-numbered computer in a pair. When you see "yy", substitute the unique number assigned to the even-numbered computer in a pair. **When you see "zz", substitute the number assigned to the computer that you are currently working at, regardless of whether it is odd or even.***

SCENARIO

You are a network administrator for the Baldwin Museum of Science. The Active Directory configuration of your company consists of two domains configured in a parent–child relationship. Both domains are using the Microsoft Windows 2000 native functional level. The forest is in the Windows 2000 functional level. The first domain controller in your domain is the only global catalog server; it holds all of the Flexible Single Master Operations (FSMO) roles.

Five domain controllers are on your network. All of your domain controllers run Windows Server 2008, Enterprise Edition. Three domain controllers are in the parent domain, and two domain controllers are in the child domain. Also, 500 client computers are running Windows XP Professional. Another 200 client computers are running Windows Vista, Enterprise Edition.

Your manager is concerned that the existing global catalog server is a single point of failure for your company. She does not want users to be unable to log on if the global catalog server is not online. She has also asked you to run some tests to explore the implications of moving to the Windows Server 2008 domain and forest functional level. During this lab, you will perform several tasks.

After completing this lab, you will be able to:

- Convert a domain from Windows Server 2003 to Windows Server 2008 domain functional level.

- Convert a forest from Windows 2000 to Windows Server 2008 forest functional level.

- Diagnose logon failures related to global catalog server outages.

- Enable universal group membership caching.

- Determine FSMO role holders using ntdsutil and dcdiag.

- Verify that global catalog records are registered on the Domain Name System (DNS) server.

- Determine whether an attribute is replicated in the global catalog.

Estimated lesson time: 160 minutes

Project 4.1	The Global Catalog and the Windows Server 2008 Domain Functional Level
Overview	Your manager wants to know what would happen if the global catalog server in your environment fails. She has asked you to run some tests on your test network to determine the effect of an unavailable global catalog server on the success or failure of network logons. In addition, she would like you to test the implications of raising the domain and forest functional levels to Windows Server 2008.
Outcomes	After completing this exercise, you will know how to: • Raise the domain functional level. • Raise the forest functional level. • Test client dependency on the global catalog server.
Completion time	40 minutes
Precautions	On the odd-numbered computer (RWDC*xx*), log on using administrative credentials in the domain*xx*.local domain. On the even-numbered computer (RWDC*yy*), log on using administrative credentials in the child*yy*.domain*xx*.local domain. You must complete the Lab Cleanup exercises from Lab 3 before performing these exercises.

■ PART A: Raise the Parent Domain Functional Level

1. Press Ctrl+Alt+Delete on the RWDC*xx* computer and log on with administrative credentials to the domain*xx*.local domain. Your username will be Administrator. The password will be MSPress#1 or the password that your instructor or lab proctor has assigned to you. Close the Server Manager window when it is displayed automatically.

2. Open the Active Directory Domains And Trusts console.

3. Right-click the domain*xx*.local node and then click Raise Domain Functional Level. The Raise Domain Functional Level dialog box is displayed.

4. In the dropdown selection box, click Windows Server 2008 and then click Raise. A message box is displayed.

5. Read the message and then confirm it by clicking OK. A second message box is displayed, indicating that the domain functional level has been raised.

6. Click OK.

Question 1	*Would you be able to raise the forest functional level to Windows Server 2008 at this point?*

7. Log off of the computer.

■ PART B: Raise the Child Domain Functional Level

1. Press Ctrl+Alt+Delete on the RWDC*yy* computer and log on with administrative credentials to the child*yy*.domain*xx*.local domain. Your username will be Administrator. The password will be MSPress#1 or the password that your instructor or lab proctor has assigned to you. Close the Server Manager window when it is displayed automatically.

2. Open the Active Directory Domains And Trusts console.

3. Right-click the child*yy*.domain*xx*.local node and then click Raise Domain Functional Level. The Raise Domain Functional Level dialog box is displayed.

4. In the dropdown selection box, click Windows Server 2008 and then click Raise. A message box is displayed.

5. Read the message and then confirm it by clicking OK. A second message box will be displayed, indicating that the domain functional level has been raised.

6. Click OK.

Question 2	*Would you be able to raise the forest functional level to Windows Server 2008 at this point? Why or why not?*

7. Close Active Directory Domains And Trusts and log off of the computer.

■ PART C: Raise the Forest Functional Level

1. Press Ctrl+Alt+Delete on the RWDC*xx* computer and log on with administrative credentials to the domain*xx*.local domain. Your username will be Administrator. The password will be MSPress#1 or the password that your instructor or lab proctor has assigned to you. Close the Server Manager window when it is displayed automatically.

2. Open the Active Directory Domains And Trusts console.

3. Right-click the top-level node Active Directory Domains And Trusts [RWDC*xx*.domain*xx*.local] and then click Raise Forest Functional Level. The Raise Forest Functional Level dialog box is displayed.

4. In the dropdown selection box, click Windows Server 2008 and then click Raise. A message box is displayed.

5. Read the message and then confirm it by clicking OK. A second message box is displayed, indicating that the forest functional level has been raised.

6. Click OK.

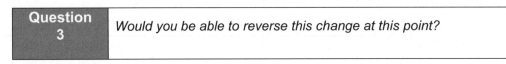

Question 3	Would you be able to reverse this change at this point?

7. Close Active Directory Domains And Trusts and log off of the computer.

■ PART D: Simulate a Global Catalog Failure

1. Press Ctrl+Alt+Delete on the RWDC*xx* computer and log on with administrative credentials to the domain*xx*.local domain. Your username will be Administrator. The password will be MSPress#1 or the password that your instructor or lab proctor has assigned to you. Close the Server Manager window when it is displayed automatically.

2. Open the Active Directory Sites And Services console.

3. Click Sites, click Default-First-Site-Name, click Servers, and then click RWDC*xx*. Right-click NTDS Settings and select Properties. The NTDS Settings Properties dialog box is displayed.

4. Remove the checkbox next to Global Catalog. A warning message will be displayed indicating that clients will be unable to log on if they cannot locate a global catalog. Click OK to acknowledge the error and then click OK again to save your changes.

5. If you configured the RODC*xx* and/or the SCDC*xx* domain controllers in Lab 2 and both servers are currently running, repeat steps 3 and 4 for both of these servers.

6. Log off of the computer.

■ PART E: Test the Global Catalog Failure

1. On the odd-numbered computer, attempt to log on using the UPN for student*xx*@domain*xx*.local. The password will be MSPress#1 or the password that your instructor or lab proctor has assigned to you.

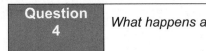

Question 4	What happens at this point?

2. On the even-numbered computer, attempt to log on using the UPN for child*yy*student*yy*@child*yy*.domain*xx*.local. The password will be MSPress#1 or the password that your instructor or lab proctor has assigned to you.

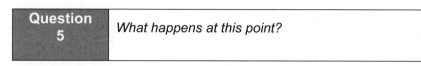

Question 5	What happens at this point?

■ PART F: Resolve the Global Catalog Failure

1. Press Ctrl+Alt+Delete on the RWDC*xx* computer and log on as the default Administrator account in the domain*xx*.local domain. Your username will be Administrator. The password will be MSPress#1 or the password that your instructor or lab proctor has assigned to you. Close the Server Manager window when it is displayed automatically.

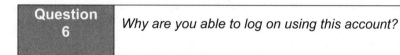

Question 6	Why are you able to log on using this account?

2. Open the Active Directory Sites And Services console.

3. Click Sites, click Default-First-Site-Name, click Servers, and then click RWDC*xx*. Right-click NTDS Settings and select Properties. The NTDS Settings Properties dialog box is displayed.

4. Place a check in the checkbox next to Global Catalog and click OK.

5. If you configured the RODC*xx* and/or the SCDC*xx* domain controllers in Lab 2, repeat steps 3 and 4 for both of these servers.

6. Log off of the computer.

■ PART G: Test the Availability of the Global Catalog

NOTE	Wait at least 5 minutes after performing Part F before you attempt this portion of the project.

1. On the odd-numbered computer, attempt to log on using the UPN for student*xx*@domain*xx*.local. The password will be MSPress#1 or the password that your instructor or lab proctor has assigned to you.

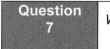

Question 7	What happens at this point?

2. On the even-numbered computer, attempt to log on using the UPN for child*yy*student*yy*@child*yy*.domain*xx*.local. The password will be MSPress#1 or the password that your instructor or lab proctor has assigned to you.

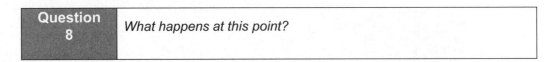

Question 8	What happens at this point?

Project 4.2	Enabling Universal Group Membership Caching
Overview	Your manager wants to know if the universal group membership caching feature will alleviate her concerns about user logon dependency on the global catalog. You decide to run an experiment in your test lab to see how universal group membership caching works in the event of a global catalog failure.
Outcomes	After completing this exercise, you will know how to: • Enable universal group membership caching.
Completion time	25 minutes
Precautions	Some of the steps in this exercise should only be performed on one computer in each pair. You will be informed which computer, odd or even, to use in the first step of each portion of this exercise.

■ PART A: Enabling Universal Group Membership Caching

1. Press Ctrl+Alt+Delete on the RWDC*xx* computer and log on as the default administrator of the local computer. Your username will be Administrator. The password will be MSPress#1 or the password that your instructor or lab proctor has assigned to you. Close the Server Manager window when it is displayed automatically.

2. Open the Active Directory Sites And Services console.

3. In the left pane, click Sites, and then click Default-First-Site-Name. Right-click NTDS Site Settings and click Properties. The NTDS Site Settings Properties dialog box is displayed.

4. Place a checkmark next to Enable Universal Membership Group Caching and click OK.

5. Force Active Directory replication using any one of the techniques you learned in previous labs.

■ PART B: Logging on with Universal Group Membership Caching Enabled

1. On the even-numbered computer, log on to the child domain using the UPN for child*yy*student*yy*@child*yy*.domain*xx*.local.

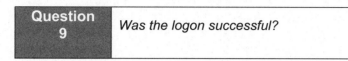

Question 9	Was the logon successful?

2. Log off of the even-numbered computer.

■ PART C: Simulating a Global Catalog Failure

1. Press Ctrl+Alt+Delete on the RWDC*xx* computer and log on with administrative credentials to the domain*xx*.local domain. Your username will be Administrator. The password will be MSPress#1 or the password that your instructor or lab proctor assigns to you. Close the Server Manager window when it is displayed automatically.

2. Open the Active Directory Sites And Services console.

3. Click Sites, click Default-First-Site-Name, click Servers, and then click RWDC*xx*. Right-click NTDS Settings and select Properties. The NTDS Settings Properties dialog box is displayed.

4. Remove the checkbox next to Global Catalog and click OK.

5. If you configured the RODC*xx* and/or the SCDC*xx* domain controllers in Lab 2, repeat steps 3 and 4 for both of these servers.

6. Log off of the computer.

■ PART D: Testing User Logon Without the Global Catalog

1. On the even-numbered computer, log on to the child domain using the UPN for child*yy*student*yy*@child*yy*.domain*xx*.local.

Question 10	Did this logon succeed, even though the global catalog server is not available?

2. Log off of the even-numbered computer.

3. On the odd-numbered computer, attempt to log onto the child domain using the UPN for child*yy*student*yy*@child*yy*.domain*xx*.local.

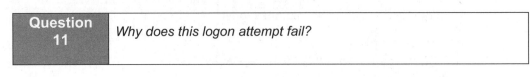

Question 11	*Why does this logon attempt fail?*

4. Ensure that you are logged off of the odd-numbered computer.

5. Configure the odd-numbered computers (RWDC*xx*, RODC*xx*, SCDC*xx*) as global catalog servers.

6. Disable universal group membership caching for the Default-First-Site-Name site.

Project 4.3	Working with Flexible Single Master Operations Roles
Overview	Your manager tells you that the computer holding the schema operations master role must be replaced soon. She asks you to transfer that role to another server for a short period until a new domain controller can be put in place.
Outcomes	After completing this exercise, you will know how to: • Transfer a FSMO role to another server.
Completion time	15 minutes
Precautions	N/A

■ PART A: Viewing Operations Masters

First, you must determine which server holds the schema operations master role.

1. On the even-numbered computer, log on as the default administrator of the child*yy*.domain*xx*.local domain.

2. Click the Start button, key **ntdsutil**, and then press Enter.

3. Key **roles** and then press Enter.

4. Key **connections** and then press Enter.

5. Key **connect to server RWDC*xx*.domain*xx*.local** and then press Enter.

6. Key **quit** and then press Enter.

7. Key **select operation target** and then press Enter.

8. Key **list roles for connected server** and then press Enter. Review the output information.

Question 12	What FSMO roles are assigned to the odd-numbered computer?

9. Key **quit**.

10. Key **connections** and then press Enter.

11. Key **connect to server RWDC*yy*.child*yy*.domain*xx*.local** and then press Enter.

12. Key **quit** and then press Enter.

13. Key **select operation target** and then press Enter.

14. Key **list roles for connected server** and then press Enter.

Question 13	What FSMO roles are assigned to the even-numbered computer?

15. Key **quit** to return to the command-prompt window.

16. Close the command-prompt window and log off of the even-numbered computer.

■ PART B: Transferring the Schema Master to a Different Domain Controller

Next, you must move the schema operations master to another domain controller. In a production environment, you should always leave the schema master FSMO role on a domain controller in the forest root domain. You are performing this activity to get the experience of transferring an operations master role with ntdsutil. To complete this exercise, the user account that you use must be a member of Schema Admins or have user rights that allow schema management. The default domain administrator of the parent domain has the appropriate rights.

1. On the odd-numbered computer, log on as the default administrator of the domain*xx*.local domain.

2. Click the Start button, key **ntdsutil**, and then press Enter.

3. Key **roles** and then press Enter.

4. Key **conncctions** and then press Enter.

5. Key **connect to server RWDC*yy*.child*yy*.domain*xx*.local** and then press Enter.

6. Key **quit** and then press Enter.

7. Key **transfer schema master** and then press Enter. A Role Transfer Confirmation dialog message is displayed.

8. Read the message and then click Yes.

9. Review the output of the ntdsutil window to confirm that the even-numbered computer is now listed as the schema operations master.

10. Key **quit** to return to the command-prompt window.

11. Close the command-prompt window and log off of the odd-numbered computer.

■ PART C: Transferring the Schema Master to the New Domain Controller

Assume that the new server has replaced the old server. Now, you must transfer the schema operations master role back to the "new" server. To complete this exercise, the user account that you use must be a member of Schema Admins or have user rights that allow schema management. The default domain administrator of the parent domain has the appropriate rights.

1. On the even-numbered computer, log on as the default administrator of the domain*xx*.local domain.

2. Click the Start button, key **ntdsutil**, and then press Enter.

3. Key **roles** and then press Enter.

4. Key **connections** and then press Enter.

5. Key **connect to server RWDC*xx*.domain*xx*.local** and then press Enter.

6. Key **quit** and then press Enter.

7. Key **transfer schema master** and then press Enter. A Role Transfer Confirmation dialog message is displayed.

8. Read the message and then click Yes.

9. Review the output of the ntdsutil window to confirm that the odd-numbered computer is now listed as the schema operations master.

10. Key **quit** to return to the command-prompt window.

11. Close the command-prompt window and log off of the odd-numbered computer.

LAB REVIEW QUESTIONS

Completion time	15 minutes

1. In your own words, describe what you learned by completing this lab.

2. You are the network administrator for an Active Directory domain that has five domain controllers. The domain functional level is set to Windows Server 2003. Only one domain controller is configured as a global catalog server. If that global catalog server fails, will it prevent users from logging onto the network?

3. How many FSMO roles would you find in an Active Directory forest that has one parent domain and two child domains?

LAB CHALLENGE 4.1	USING THE DNS CONSOLE TO VERIFY GLOBAL CATALOG RECORDS ON THE DNS SERVER
Overview	Another administrator says he is having trouble resolving some issues with a global catalog server that he just removed from the network. He wants you to check on the global catalog servers that are registered with the DNS server. You decide to use the DNS console to check these records.
Outcomes	After completing this exercise, you will know how to: • Verify DNS records for global catalog servers.
Completion time	10 minutes
Precautions	N/A

On the odd-numbered computer, use the DNS console to locate global catalog SRV records in the domain.

LAB CHALLENGE 4.2	VERIFYING FSMO ROLE HOLDERS WITH DCDIAG
Overview	Your manager tells you that another administrator transferred various FSMO roles as an experiment. She asks you to verify which servers hold all of the FSMO roles. You want to use DCDiag to output the FSMO role holders to a file named FSMO.txt on the C:\ drive.
Outcomes	After completing this exercise, you will know how to: • Use DCDiag to list the FSMO role holders.
Completion time	10 minutes
Precautions	N/A

Locate the domain controllers that hold the FSMO roles in the enterprise by using the DCDiag tool, which is used to perform diagnostic tests on Windows Server 2008 computers. Use the command dcdiag /? to help you figure out the proper syntax.

LAB CHALLENGE 4.3	DETERMINING WHETHER AN ATTRIBUTE IS REPLICATED IN THE GLOBAL CATALOG
Overview	Your manager wants to know if the sIDHistory attribute is maintained in the global catalog server.
Outcomes	After completing this exercise, you will know how to: • View the properties of an Active Directory attribute.
Completion time	20 minutes
Precautions	To use the Active Directory Schema snap-in, you must register it by keying regsvr32 schmmgmt.dll at the command line.

Use the Active Directory Schema snap-in and locate the properties of the sIDHistory attribute.

LAB A
TROUBLESHOOTING

BEFORE YOU BEGIN

Troubleshooting Lab A is a practical application of the knowledge you have acquired from Labs 1 through 4. Troubleshooting Lab A is divided into two sections: "Reviewing a Network" and "Troubleshooting a Break Scenario." In the "Reviewing a Network" section, you will review and assess a Windows Server 2008 Active Directory network for City Power & Light. In the "Troubleshooting a Break Scenario" section, you will troubleshoot a particular break scenario. In this section, your instructor or lab assistant has changed your computer configuration, causing it to "break." Your task in this section will be to apply your acquired skills to troubleshoot and resolve the break.

REVIEWING A NETWORK

In this portion of Troubleshooting Lab A, you are the network administrator for City Power & Light (www.cpandl.com). City Power & Light has five different locations named Central, Northwest, Northeast, Southwest, and Southeast. The Central location has 500 client computers and two network servers. Each of the Northwest and Northeast locations has approximately 75 client computers and one server computer. Each of the Southwest and Southeast locations has 100 client computers and one network server. Figure A-1 illustrates the company's network infrastructure.

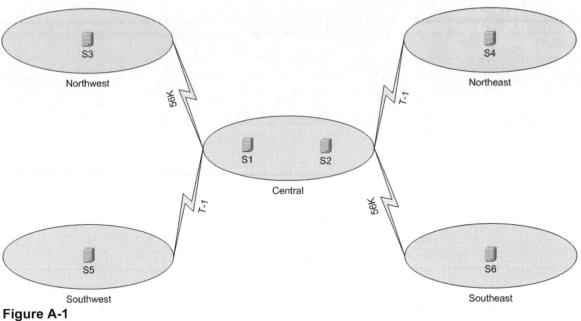

Figure A-1
City Power & Light network infrastructure

S1, S2, S3, S4, S5, and S6 are servers on the City Power & Light network. All of these servers run Windows Server 2008, Standard Edition. All client computers run Windows XP Professional. All computers are configured in a single workgroup named WORKGROUP.

Andy Ruth, director of City Power & Light, asks you to design an Active Directory infrastructure for the company. He wants everyone to have single sign-on capabilities to every server in the network. He tells you that all users use the same applications and have roughly equivalent configurations. He thinks that the 56 Kbps links are a little slow for the company, and he wants to have control over traffic sent across those links. However, the T-1 links can handle more traffic without a problem. Andy tells you that no special security needs require isolating any of the remote locations from the central location.

Based on what you know about the City Power & Light network infrastructure, answer each of the following questions. Include an explanation of why you chose each answer, based the information provided and your understanding of the concepts presented.

1. How many forests do you configure for City Power & Light?

2. How many domains do you recommend?

3. What is the minimum number of sites to configure?

4. Where would you place global catalog servers or enable universal group membership caching?

5. After you complete your initial configuration, Andy decides that he wants the ability to control replication intervals over all WAN links. How do you change the configuration to accommodate this new request?

6. How do you assign the operations master roles in the Central location?

7. Which domain controller do you configure as the global catalog server in the Central location?

8. Sketch your proposed configuration based on your answers to the previous questions.

TROUBLESHOOTING A BREAK SCENARIO

In this portion of Troubleshooting Lab A, you must resolve a "break" scenario that was introduced by your instructor or lab assistant. The computers you are assigned to fix are set up in pairs. When you are troubleshooting this issue, consider that the two computers you are troubleshooting are configured as shown in Figure A-2. This is the expected configuration for each group of two computers. Any number of configuration errors may be present in your actual lab environment.

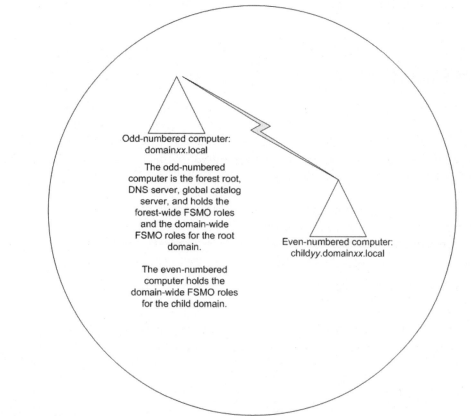

Figure A-2
Computer configuration

> | | *Do not proceed with break instructions until you receive guidance from your instructor. Your instructor or lab assistant will linform you which break scenario you will be performing (Break Scenario 1 or Break Scenario 2) and which computer to use. Your instructor or lab assistant may also have special instructions. Consult with your instructor before proceeding.* |
> | :---: | :--- |
> | **NOTE** | |

Break Scenario 1

Logging on using the even-numbered computer to the parent domain takes a long time, particularly the "Applying computer settings" portion of the boot sequence. Administrators are unable to synchronize the child domain using the repadmin/syncall command. Active Directory administrative consoles do not appear to function properly on the even-numbered computer.

As you resolve the configuration issues, record the following information:

- Description of the issue
- A list of all the steps taken to diagnose the problem, even the ones that did not work
- Description of the problem
- Description of the solution
- List of the resources that you used to solve this problem

Break Scenario 2

Administrators are unable to synchronize the replication connection from the even-numbered computer to the odd-numbered computer in the Active Directory Sites And Services console. Also, administrators are unable to use repadmin to synchronize the child domain. Administrators *are* able to synchronize the replication connection from the odd-numbered computer to the even-numbered computer

As you resolve the configuration issues, record the following information:

- Description of the issue
- A list of all the steps taken to diagnose the problem, even the ones that did not work
- Description of the problem
- Description of the solution
- List of the resources that you used to solve this problem

LAB 5
CREATING AND MANAGING USERS AND GROUPS

This lab contains the following projects and activities:

Project 5.1   Creating Administrative Accounts

Project 5.2   Testing Administrative Access

Project 5.3   Configuring Groups and Permissions

Project 5.4   Using dsadd to Add a User Account

Lab Review Questions

Lab Challenge 5.1   Using dsadd to Add a User Account to the Users Container

Lab Challenge 5.2   Changing the UPN Suffix with LDIFDE

BEFORE YOU BEGIN

Lab 5 assumes that you have completed the setup process as specified in the setup document and that your computer has connectivity to other lab computers and the Internet. Lab 5 also assumes that you have completed the nonoptional exercises in the previous labs. Specifically, Lab 5 assumes the following:

- The even-numbered computer (RWDC*yy*) must be configured to use the odd-numbered computer (RWDC*xx*) as its preferred DNS server, as explained in Lab 1, Project 1.4.
- Active Directory is installed on the odd-numbered computer (RWDC*xx*), as described in Lab 2, Project 2.1 and Project 2.2.
- Active Directory is installed on the even-numbered computer (RWDC*yy*), as described in Lab 2, Project 2.5.

> **NOTE**
>
> *In this lab, you will see the characters xx, yy, and zz. These directions assume that students are working in pairs, and that each student has a number. One number is odd and the other number is even. For example, the first student pair will consist of RWDC01 as the first odd-numbered computer and RWDC02 as the first even-numbered computer, RWDC03 and RWDC04 as the second student pair, and RWDC05 and RWDC06 as the third student pair. When you see "xx" in this manual, substitute the unique number assigned to the odd-numbered computer in a pair. When you see "yy", substitute the unique number assigned to the even-numbered computer in a pair.* **When you see "zz", substitute the number assigned to the computer that you are currently working at, regardless of whether it is odd or even.**

SCENARIO

You are the network administrator of Adventure Works. Adventure Works has a multiple-domain Active Directory forest. You manage all network operations. In the near future, you will add network administrators to support your organization. Before you begin to assign responsibilities to these new administrators, you want to be sure that you understand what tasks built-in administrative accounts allow you to perform. You do not want to assign these new administators more rights than necessary to perform their assigned roles.

In addition to assigning roles appropriately, you must develop an administrative hierarchy. You know that the company will have many different administrators, and you do not want to add them directly into the domain local or built-in groups. You want to separate the administrative hierarchy so that you can manage groups of administrators and groups of permissions. During this lab, you will perform several tasks.

After completing this lab, you will be able to:

■ Create administrative user accounts.

■ Change primary group memberships.

■ Identify which built-in administrative groups have the permissions necessary to create sites, create and manager users, view the Active Directory schema, and modify the Active Directory schema.

■ Create global and universal groups and use them to assign permissions to user accounts.

■ Use dsadd to add users and organizational units (OUs).

■ Make changes to user accounts with LDAP Data Interchange Format Directory Exchange (LDIFDE).

Estimated lesson time: 130 minutes

Project 5.1	Creating Administrative Accounts
Overview	You are planning to assign new administrators to the built-in groups to create sites and users and to access the Active Directory schema. You must determine which types of built-in groups give the appropriate levels of access. Before you do this, you must create test user accounts for your experiments.
Outcomes	After completing this exercise, you will know how to: • Create a user account.
Completion time	20 minutes
Precautions	Part A and Part C should be performed on the odd-numbered RWDC*xx* computer. Part B should be performed on the even-numbered RWDC*yy* computer. Part D should be performed on both computers.

■ PART A: Creating Administrative Accounts on the Parent Domain

1. Press Ctrl+Alt+Delete on the RWDC*xx* computer and log on as the default domain administrator of the domain*xx* domain. Your username will be Administrator. The password will be MSPress#1 or the password that your instructor or lab proctor has assigned to you. Close the Server Manager screen when it is displayed automatically.

2. To open the Active Directory Users And Computers MMC snap-in, click Start, click Administrative Tools, and then click Active Directory Users And Computers. Expand the domain object domain*xx*.local in the left window pane, if necessary.

3. In the left window pane, right-click the Users container. Click New, and then click User. The New Object–User dialog box is displayed.

4. Create a new user account named DomAdmin in the default Users container. In the Full Name text box, key **DomAdmin**.

5. Click the User Logon Name text box, key **DomAdmin**, the same name used in Step 4, and then click Next.

6. Key **MSPress#1** in the Password text box and in the Confirm Password text box.

7. Clear the User Must Change Password At Next Logon checkbox. Click Next, and then click Finish.

8. Ensure that the Users container is selected. In the right window pane of Active Directory Users And Computers, right-click DomAdmin and click Properties. The DomAdmin Properties dialog box is displayed.

9. Click the MemberOf tab. Click Add. The Select Groups dialog box is displayed.

10. Key **Domain Admins** in the Enter The Object Name To Select text box. Click OK.

11. In the DomAdmin Properties dialog box, click Domain Admins in the MemberOf selection box. Click Set Primary Group to make the primary group Domain Admins.

12. Click Domain Users in the MemberOf selection box. Click Remove to make Domain Admins the only group membership for this user account. A message about removing a user from the group text is displayed. Read the message and click Yes.

13. Click OK in the DomAdmin Properties dialog box.

14. Repeat the previous steps to create two additional accounts named SchAdmin and EntAdmin. Ensure that the SchAdmin account is a member of only the Schema Admins group and that the EntAdmin account is a member of only the Enterprise Admins group.

■ PART B: Creating Administrative Accounts on the Child Domain

1. Press Ctrl+Alt+Delete on the RWDC*yy* computer and log on as the default domain administrator of the child*yy*.domain*xx* domain. Your username will be Administrator. The password will be MSPress#1 or the password that your instructor or lab proctor has assigned to you. Close the Server Manager screen when it is displayed automatically.

2. To open the Active Directory Users And Computers MMC snap-in, click Start, click Administrative Tools, and then click Active Directory Users And Computers. Expand the domain object child*yy*.domain*xx*.local in the left window pane, if necessary.

3. In the left window pane, right-click the Users container. Click New, and then click User. The New Object–User dialog box is displayed.

4. Create a new user account named DomAdmin in the default Users container. In the Full Name text box, key **DomAdmin**.

5. Click the User Logon Name text box, key **DomAdmin**, the same name used in Step 4, and then click Next.

6. Key **MSPress#1** in the Password text box and in the Confirm Password text box.

7. Clear the User Must Change Password At Next Logon checkbox. Click Next, and then click Finish.

8. Verify that the Users container is selected. In the right window pane of Active Directory Users And Computers, right-click DomAdmin and click Properties. The DomAdmin Properties dialog box is displayed.

9. Click the MemberOf tab. Click Add. The Select Groups dialog box is displayed.

10. Key **Domain Admins** in the Enter The Object Name To Select text box. Click OK.

11. In the DomAdmin Properties dialog box, click Domain Admins in the MemberOf selection box. Click Set Primary Group to make the primary group Domain Admins.

12. Select Domain Users in the MemberOf selection box. Click Remove to make Domain Admins the only group membership for this user account. A message about removing a user from the group text is displayed. Read the message and click Yes.

13. Click OK in the DomAdmin Properties dialog box.

14. Repeat the previous steps to create two additional accounts named SchAdmin and EntAdmin. Do not configure group memberships for these accounts, because this will be done in the next part of this project using the odd-numbered computer.

■ PART C: Adding Child User Accounts to Enterprise-wide Administrative Roles

1. Press Ctrl+Alt+Delete on the odd-numbered RWDC*xx* computer and log on as the default domain administrator of the domain*xx* domain. Your username will be Administrator. The password will be MSPress#1 or the password that your instructor or lab proctor has assigned to you. Close the Server Manager screen when it is displayed automatically.

2. To open the Active Directory Users And Computers MMC snap-in, click Start, click Administrative Tools, and then click Active Directory Users And Computers. Expand the domain object domain*xx*.local in the left window pane, if necessary.

3. Verify that the Users container is selected. Right-click the Enterprise Admins group in the right window pane and then click Properties. An Enterprise Admins Properties dialog box is displayed.

4. Click the Members tab and then click Add. The Select Users, Contacts, Computers, Or Groups dialog box is displayed.

5. Click Locations. The Locations dialog box is displayed.

6. Expand the domain*xx*.local object and then expand the child*yy*.domain*xx*.local domain.

7. Click the Users container under the child domain and then click OK.

8. Key **EntAdmin** in the Enter The Object Name To Select text box in the Select Users, Contacts, Computers, Or Groups dialog box. Click Check Names. The EntAdmin user from the child domain should be displayed and underlined. Click OK.

9. Click OK on the Enterprise Admins Properties dialog box.

10. Repeat steps 1 to 9 to add the SchAdmin user account from the child*yy* domain to the Schema Admins group on the parent domain.

■ PART D: Allowing Users to Log On to Domain Controllers

> **NOTE**
>
> *You are about to allow nonadministrative users to log on to a domain controller. You are doing this only for testing purposes; you typically would not want domain users to be able to interactively (locally) log on to a domain controller.*

1. On the odd- and even-numbered computers, open the Group Policy Management Console. Expand the tree until you find Domain Controllers. Right-click the Default Domain Controllers Policy and click Edit. The Group Policy Management Editor window is displayed.

2. In the left console pane, expand Computer Configuration, expand Policies, expand Windows Settings, expand Security Settings, expand Local Policies, and then click User Rights Assignment.

3. In the right pane, double-click the Allow Logon Locally policy object. The Allow Logon Locally Properties dialog box is displayed.

4. Make sure you check the box for Define these Policy settings. Click Add User Or Group. An Add User Or Group dialog box is displayed.

5. Check to make sure Administrators is already listed. Key **Users** in the User And Group Names text box. Click OK, and then click OK again in the Allow Logon Locally Properties dialog box.

6. Close the Group Policy Management Editor and the Group Policy Management Console.

7. Log off of the odd- and even-numbered computers.

Project 5.2	Testing Administrative Access
Overview	You must now test the capabilities of each of the user accounts you created in the previous project.
Outcomes	After completing this exercise, you will know how to: • Test the privileges of Active Directory users.
Completion time	40 minutes
Precautions	Use the DomAdmin, SchAdmin, and EntAdmin administrative accounts created in Project 5.1 to complete this activity.

■ PART A: Determine Which Accounts Can Create Sites

1. Log on using the user account being tested, such as DomAdmin. On the odd-numbered RWDC*xx* computer, log onto the domain*xx* domain. On the even-numbered RWDC*yy* computer, log onto the child*yy* domain.

2. Using the Active Directory Sites And Services MMC snap-in, attempt to create a site. Try to create a unique site name with each administrative account. Record the names of the accounts that can be used to create a new site. Refer to Project 3.3 if you need directions for creating a site.

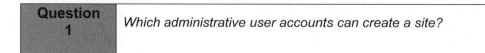

| Question 1 | Which administrative user accounts can create a site? |

3. If a site is created successfully, right-click the site name and click Delete in the left window pane of Active Directory Sites And Services. An Active Directory message is displayed. Read the message and click Yes to confirm that you want to delete the site. Another Active Directory message box is displayed. Read the message and click Yes to confirm.

4. Repeat steps 1 through 3 for the SchAdmin and EntAdmin administrative accounts.

■ PART B: Determine Which Accounts Can Create Users

1. Log on using the user account being tested, such as DomAdmin. On the odd-numbered RWDC*xx* computer, log onto the domain*xx* domain. On the even-numbered RWDC*yy* computer, log onto the child*yy* domain.

2. Using the Active Directory Users And Computers MMC snap-in, attempt to create a unique user account on the local domain. Record the names of the accounts that can be used to create new users.

3. Using Active Directory Users And Computers, attempt to create a unique user account on the opposite domain. In the left window pane of the Active Directory Users And Computers console, right-click the Active Directory Users And Computers node and click Connect To Domain. The Connect To Domain dialog box is displayed.

4. Click Browse. The Browse For Domain dialog box is displayed.

5. Select the opposite domain and click OK.

6. In the opposite domain, attempt to create a unique user account. Record the names of the accounts that can be used to create new users.

7. Repeat steps 1 through 6 for the SchAdmin and EntAdmin administrative accounts.

8. Close the Active Directory Users And Computers console and log off.

■ PART C: Determine Which Accounts Can Manage the Schema

1. On the odd-numbered RWDC*xx* computer, log on as the DomAdmin user of the domain*xx* domain. On the even-numbered RWDC*yy* computer, log on as the DomAdmin user of the child*yy* domain.

2. Click the Start button, key **regsvr32 schmmgmt.dll**, and press Enter. Click OK in the message box indicating that the registration succeeded.

3. Click the Start button, key **mmc**, and press Enter. The MMC console is displayed.

4. Click File, and then click Add/Remove Snap-in. The Add/Remove Snap-in window is displayed.

5. Click Add. The Add Standalone Snap-In dialog box is displayed.

6. Locate and click the Active Directory Schema snap-in.

7. Click Add, and then click Close. The Add/Remove Snap-In dialog box is displayed.

8. Click OK.

9. Expand the Active Directory Schema node to reveal the Classes and Attribute nodes.

10. Click Attributes. A list of schema attributes will be displayed in the right window pane.

11. Right-click the Attributes object. If you see that the option to Create Attribute is gray in the context menu, then this user account does not have the ability to modify the schema.

12. Click the File menu, and then click Save As.

13. Key **c:\schema.msc** in the File Name text box. Click Save and close the Schema console.

14. Log off of the local computer.

15. Log on as the SchAdmin user of the local domain.

16. Click Start, key **c:\schema.msc**, and press Enter. The Schema console should be displayed. If you can view the list of Active Directory Schema attributes, the user account has the ability to view the schema. You may need to enter your password again.

17. Right-click the Attributes object. If you see that the Create Attribute option is available in the context menu, the user account has the ability to modify the schema.

18. Log off and log on as the EntAdmin user. Repeat steps 16 through 18 to determine whether the EntAdmin user has the ability to view and/or modify the schema.

Project 5.3	Configuring Groups and Permissions
Overview	You must now create an administrative structure that you can use for new administrators. Group administrators into separate global groups. Then, create a universal group that can be used to give new administrators permissions equivalent to the local administrators of each domain.
Outcomes	After completing this exercise, you will know how to: <ul><li>Create group objects.</li><li>Assign permissions to a group.</li></ul>
Completion time	15 minutes
Precautions	N/A

■ PART A: Creating Global Groups

1. On the odd-numbered RWDC*xx* computer, log on as the default administrator of the domain*xx*.local domain.

2. Open the Active Directory Users And Computers console.

3. Expand the domain*xx*.local domain, and then right-click the Users container.

4. Click New, and then click Group. The New Object–Group dialog box is displayed. Notice that the Group Scope default is Global and the Group Type default is Security. Keep these default settings.

5. Key **LAdmins*xx*** in the Group Name text box and click OK.

6. On the even-numbered RWDC*yy* computer, log on as the default administrator of the child*xx* domain.

7. Open the Active Directory Users And Computers console.

8. Expand the child*yy*.domain*xx*.local domain, and then right-click the Users container.

9. Click New, and then click Group. The New Object–Group dialog box is displayed. Notice the Group Scope default is Global and the Group Type default is Security. Keep these default settings.

10. Key **LAdmins***yy* in the Group Name text box. Click OK.

■ PART B: Creating Universal Groups

1. On the odd-numbered RWDC*xx* computer, right-click the Users container.

2. Click New, and then click Group. The New Object–Group dialog box is displayed.

3. Key **LAdmins** in the Group Name text box.

4. In the Group Scope area, select the Universal radio button. Verify that the Group Type is set to Security and click OK.

5. Verify that the Users container is selected. In the right pane of Active Directory Users And Computers, right-click LAdmins, and then click Properties.

6. Click the Members tab. Click Add. The Select Users, Contacts, Computers, Or Groups dialog box is displayed.

7. Key **LAdmins***xx* in the Enter The Object Names To Select text box, and then click OK. Remember that LAdmins*xx* is a global group.

8. Click Add again. The Select Users, Contacts, Computers, Or Groups dialog box is displayed again.

9. Click Locations. The Locations dialog box is displayed.

10. Expand the parent domain, and then expand the child domain.

11. Click the Users container under the child domain, and then click OK.

12. Key **LAdmins***yy* in the Enter The Object Names To Select text box, and then click OK. Remember that LAdmins*yy* is a global group.

13. Click the Member Of tab and click Add. The Select Groups dialog box is displayed.

14. Key **Administrators** in the Enter The Object Names To Select text box. Click OK.

15. Click Add again. The Select Groups dialog box is displayed.

16. Click Locations. The Locations dialog box is displayed.

17. Expand the parent domain.

18. Click the child domain and click OK.

19. Key **Administrators** in the Enter The Object Names To Select text box, and then click OK.

20. Click OK in the LAdmins Properties dialog box.

■ PART C: Assigning Permissions Through Group Membership

1. On the odd-numbered RWDC*xx* computer, create a user acount named LocalAdmin*xx* on the parent domain. Refer to Project 5.1, Creating Administrative Accounts on the Parent Domain.

2. Make the LocalAdmin*xx* user a member of the LAdmins*xx* group.

3. On the even-numbered RWDC*yy* computer, create a user account named LocalAdmin*yy* on the child domain. Refer to Project 5.1, Creating Administrative Accounts on the Child domain.

4. Make the LocalAdmin*yy* user a member of the LAdmins*yy* group.

5. Log off and log on to each computer with its newly-created user account.

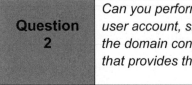

Question 2	Can you perform administrative tasks, such as creating a user account, shutting down the server, or setting the time, on the domain controllers? Explain the group membership chain that provides this user account with its current permissions.

6. Log off of both computers.

Project 5.4	Using dsadd to Add a User Account
Overview	Your organization is growing and you need to add new OUs and users.
Outcomes	After completing this exercise, you will know how to: • Create an OU from the command line. • Create a user from the command line.
Completion time	10 minutes
Precautions	N/A

■ PART A: Using dsadd to Create an OU and User in the Parent Domain

A Sales department was added to your organizational structure, and you decide to create a new OU to help you manage the resources of this new department. Additionally, a new manager, Kim Ralls, was just hired for the Sales department. You must create a user account for Kelly in the new OU. Use dsadd to add these new objects.

1. On the odd-numbered RWDC*xx* computer, log on as the default administrator of the domain*xx* domain.

2. Open a command prompt window.

3. Key **dsadd ou ou=Sales,dc=domain*xx*,dc=local –desc Lab5** in the command prompt window, and then press Enter.

4. Key **dsadd user cn=Kim,ou=Sales,dc=domain*xx*,dc=local –pwd MSPress#1 – samid KimR –upn Kim@domain*xx*.local** in the command prompt window. Press Enter.

5. Open the Active Directory Users And Computers console and verify that the Sales OU exists and that the Kim user accounts exists inside the OU.

■ PART B: Using dsadd to Create an OU and User in the Child Domain

A Service department was added to your organizational structure, and you decide to create a new OU to help you manage the resources of this new department. Additionally, a new manager, Ajay Solanki, was just hired for the Service department. You must create a user account for Jeff in the new OU. Use dsadd to add these new objects.

1. On the even-numbered RWDC*yy* computer, log on as the default administrator of the child*yy* domain.

2. Open a command-prompt window.

3. Key **dsadd ou ou=Service,dc=child*yy*,dc=domain*xx*,dc=local –desc Lab5** in the command-prompt window. Press Enter.

4. Key **dsadd user cn=Ajay,ou=Service,dc=child*yy*,dc=domain*xx*,dc=local –pwd MSPress#1 –samid AjayS –upn Ajay@child*yy*.domain*xx*.local** in the command-prompt window. Press Enter.

5. Open the Active Directory Users And Computers console and verify that the Service OU exists and that the Ajay user accounts exists inside the OU.

LAB REVIEW QUESTIONS

Completion time   15 minutes

1. In your own words, describe what you learned by completing this lab.

2. Name a task that a member of Schema Admins cannot perform that a member of Enterprise Admins or Domain Admins can perform.

3. What command must you run before you can add the Active Directory Schema console as a snap-in to the Microsoft Management Console?

4. What type of administrative membership allows you to add attributes and object classes to the Active Directory database?

LAB CHALLENGE 5.1	USING DSADD TO ADD A USER ACCOUNT TO THE USERS CONTAINER
Overview	Lolan Song and Mike Nash are new employees. Use dsadd to create user accounts for them in the appropriate domain.
Outcomes	After completing this exercise, you will know how to: • Use dsadd to create a user account.
Completion time	10 minutes
Precautions	N/A

Task 1: On the odd-numbered RWDC*xx* computer, use dsadd to create a user account for Lolan Song in the Users container of the domain*xx* domain. Lolan's username should be Lolan, and her pre–Windows 2000 username should by LolanS. Her User Principal Name (UPN) should be lolan@domain*xx*.com. Set her password to MSPress#1.

Task 2: On the even-numbered RWDC*yy* computer, use dsadd to create a user account for Mike Nash in the Users container of the child*yy* domain. Mike's user logon name should be Mike, and his pre–Windows 2000 user logon name should be MikeN. Set his password to MSPress#1. His UPN should be mike@child*yy*.domain*xx*.local.

LAB CHALLENGE 5.2	CHANGING THE UPN SUFFIX WITH LDIFDE
Overview	Lolan and Mike say that they need the UPN suffix contoso.com. They want to be able to log on as Lolan@contoso.com and Mike@contoso.com, respectively.
Outcomes	Use LDIFDE to modify user accounts.
Completion time	20 minutes
Precautions	N/A

Modify the accounts you created for Lolan and Mike using an LDIFDE file to change the UPN. Create one file to be used on the odd-numbered RWDC*xx* computer to modify Lolan's account. Create another file to be used on the even-numbered RWDC*yy* computer to modify Mike's account.

LAB 6
EMPLOYING SECURITY CONCEPTS

This lab contains the following projects and activities:

Project 6.1	Using Naming Standards and Secure Passwords
Project 6.2	Employing Administrator Account Security
Project 6.3	Delegating Administrative Responsibility
Lab Review Questions	
Lab Challenge 6.1	Using dsmove
Lab Challenge 6.2	Moving Objects with ADMT

BEFORE YOU BEGIN

Lab 6 assumes that you have completed the setup process as specified in the setup document and that your computer has connectivity to other lab computers and the Internet. Lab 6 also assumes that you have completed the nonoptional exercises in the previous labs. Specifically, Lab 6 assumes the following:

- The even-numbered computer (RWDC*yy*) must be configured to use the odd-numbered computer (RWDC*xx*) as its preferred DNS server, as explained in Lab 1, Project 1.4.
- Active Directory is installed on the odd-numbered computer (RWDC*xx*), as described in Lab 2, Project 2.1 and Project 2.2.

- Active Directory is installed on the even-numbered computer (RWDC*yy*), as described in Lab 2, Project 2.5.
- Users have the right to log on to domain controllers, as described in Lab 5, Project 5.1.

NOTE

In this lab, you will see the characters xx, yy, and zz. These directions assume that students are working in pairs, and that each student has a number. One number is odd and the other number is even. For example, the first student pair will consist of RWDC01 as the first odd-numbered computer and RWDC02 as the first even-numbered computer, RWDC03 and RWDC04 as the second student pair, and RWDC05 and RWDC06 as the third student pair. When you see "xx" in this manual, substitute the unique number assigned to the odd-numbered computer in a pair. When you see "yy", substitute the unique number assigned to the even-numbered computer in a pair. **When you see "zz", substitute the number assigned to the computer that you are currently working at, regardless of whether it is odd or even.**

SCENARIO

You are a network administrator of Adventure Works, which has a single Active Directory domain model with four sites named Greece, Malaysia, Thailand, and Arizona. The Arizona site has three domain controllers, and each of the other sites has one domain controller. The domain uses Active Directory–integrated Domain Name System (DNS), and all domain controllers have the DNS service installed.

The forest root domain is named adventure-works.com. Adventure Works headquarters is located in Tempe, Arizona. The company also has locations on Penang Island in Malaysia, Samui Island in Thailand, and Santorini Island in Greece.

The Tempe location has three domain controllers and 250 user accounts. The main administrative functions are performed at this location. Top-level organizational units (OUs) include Accounting, Marketing, and Operations. The Accounting OU has two child OUs: Accounts Payable and Accounts Receivable. The Marketing OU has two child OUs: Sales and Customer Service. The Production OU has three child OUs: Penang, Samui, and Santorini.

Recently, a consulting group performed an audit on the adventure-works.com domain. The consulting group recommended several organizational and security changes. Your manager asked you to perform the following tasks.

After completing this lab, you will be able to:

- Implement a standard naming scheme for user accounts throughout the entire company.

- Educate users about configuring secure passwords.

- Educate other administrators about reducing administrative account exposure.

- Delegate permissions appropriately to department managers.

- Implement user-naming standards.

- Use the runas utility.

- Use the Delegation of Control Wizard.

- Move OUs and user accounts.

Estimated lesson time: 120 minutes

Project 6.1	Using Naming Standards and Secure Passwords
Overview	Company policy states that each employee's user account name must be created from the first letter of the employee's first name, the employee's entire last name, and the employee's unique identification number. All employee passwords will be complex.
Outcomes	After completing this exercise, you will know how to: • Create a normal user account.
Completion time	5 minutes
Precautions	N/A

1. Press Ctrl+Alt+Delete on the RWDC*xx* computer and log on as the default domain administrator of the domain*xx* domain. Your username will be Administrator. The password will be MSPress#1 or the password that your instructor or lab proctor has assigned to you. Close the Server Manager screen if it is displayed automatically.

2. Use the Active Directory Users And Computers console to create a user account based on your name in the Users container. Use the naming standard described in the scenario for this project. Substitute the odd-numbered computer number for the employee identification number. For example, a user named Reed Koch who is using Computer01 would have the following values:

   • **First Name: Reed**
   • **Last Name: Koch**
   • **Full Name: Reed Koch**
   • **Logon Name: RKoch01**
   • **Password: MSPress#1**
   • **User Must Change Password at Next Logon: Not selected**

3. On the even-numbered computer, log on as the default administrator of the child*yy* domain.

4. Use the Active Directory Users And Computers console to create a user account based on your name in the Users container. Use the naming standards described in the scenario for this project. Substitute the even-numbered computer number for the employee identification number. For example, a user named Brannon Jones who is using Computer02 would have the logon name BJones02. The password should be MSPress#1. Clear the User Must Change Password At Next Logon checkbox.

5. Log off of both computers.

Project 6.2	Employing Administrator Account Security
Overview	You must demonstrate the various methods for using the runas utility to allow administrators to reduce the exposure of administrative accounts.
Outcomes	After completing this exercise, you will know how to: • Launch commands using the runas utility.
Completion time	20 minutes
Precautions	Use the DomAdmin, SchAdmin, and EntAdmin administrative accounts created in Project 5.1 to complete this activity.

■ PART A: Using Runas from the Command Prompt

1. Log on to each computer using the accounts that you created in Project 6.1.

2. Open the Active Directory Users And Computers console.

3. Try to reset your password. Click the Users container in the left window pane. In the right window pane, right-click your user account and click Reset Password. A Reset Password dialog box is displayed. Key **MSPress#1** or the password that has been assigned to you in both of the password boxes. Click OK. A message box is displayed. Read the message and click OK.

Question 1	Were you able to reset your password?

4. Close the Active Directory Users And Computers console.

5. On the odd-numbered computer, open a command-prompt window. Key **runas /user:administrator@domain*xx*.local "mmc dsa.msc"**. Press Enter.

6. On the even-numbered computer, open a command-prompt window. Key **runas /user:administrator@child*yy*.domain*xx*.local "mmc dsa.msc"**. Press Enter.

7. When you are prompted for the password, key **MSPress#1** or the password that has been assigned to you. Press Enter. Wait a few seconds and the Active Directory Users And Computers console will be displayed.

8. Try to reset your password. Click the Users container in the left window pane. In the right window pane, right-click your user account and click Reset Password. The Reset Password dialog box is displayed. Key **MSPress#1** or the password that has been assigned to you in the password boxes. Click OK. A message box is displayed.

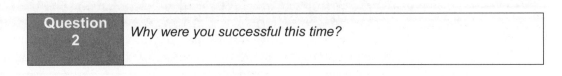

9. Click OK.

10. Close the Active Directory Users And Computers console and the command-prompt window.

■ PART B: Creating and Using a Runas Shortcut

You want to create a shortcut on your desktop that will allow you to easily manage your domains and forest without requiring you to log off when using your domain user account.

1. On either computer, find an area of the desktop where there are no icons and right-click that area.

2. Click New, and then click Shortcut. A Create Shortcut Wizard is displayed.

3. Key **runas /user:administrator@domain.xx.local "mmc domain.msc"** in the Type The Location Of The Item text box. Click Next.

4. Key **Domains and Trusts** in the Type A Name For This Shortcut text box. Click Finish.

5. Double-click the icon on the desktop that you just created. A command-prompt window is displayed.

6. Key **MSPress#1** or the password that has been assigned to you. Press Enter. The Active Directory Domains And Trusts console is displayed.

7. Close the console.

■ PART C: Attempting to Run Multiple Runas Consoles Simultaneously

You want to see if you can run multiple consoles simultaneously with the runas utility.

1. On either computer, click the Start button.

2. Key **runas /user:administrator@domain.xx.local "mmc dsa.msc"**. Press Enter. A command-prompt window is displayed.

3. Key **MSPress#1** or the password that has been assigned to you in the command-prompt window. Press Enter. The Active Directory Users And Computers console is displayed.

4. Click the Start button again.

5. Key **runas /user:administrator@domain*xx*.local "mmc dssite.msc"**. Press Enter. A command-prompt window is displayed.

6. Key **MSPress#1** or the password that has been assigned to you in the command-prompt window. Press Enter. The Active Directory Sites And Services console is displayed.

7. Click the Start button again.

8. Key **runas /user:administrator@domain*xx*.local "mmc domain.msc"**. Press Enter. A command-prompt window is displayed.

9. Key **MSPress#1** or the password that has been assigned to you in the command-prompt window. Press Enter. The Active Directory Domains And Trusts console is displayed.

10. Close all open consoles and log off of the computer.

Project 6.3	Delegating Administrative Responsibility
Overview	You must assign the ability to reset passwords to the manager of a new department.
Outcomes	After completing this exercise, you will know how to: • Delegate permissions within Active Directory.
Completion time	25 minutes
Precautions	N/A

■ PART A: Delegating Control on the Parent Domain

1. On the odd-numbered computer, log on as the default administrator of the domain*xx* domain.

2. Open a command-prompt window and key the following three commands to create user accounts that you will delegate limited permissions to:

    • **dsadd user cn=User1,cn=Users,dc=domain*xx*,dc=local –samid User1 –upn user1@domain*xx*.local –pwd MSPress#1**

    • **dsadd user cn=User2,cn=Users,dc=domain*xx*,dc=local –samid User2 –upn user2@domain*xx*.local –pwd MSPress#1**

    • **dsadd user cn=Manager,cn=Users,dc=domain*xx*,dc=local –samid Manager –upn manager@domain*xx*.local –pwd MSPress#1**

3. Open the Active Directory Users And Computers console.

4. Right-click the domain*xx*.local object in the left pane. Click New, and then click Organizational Unit. A New Object–Organizational Unit dialog box is displayed.

5. Key **Mgmt1** in the Name text box, and then click OK.

6. In the left pane of the Active Directory Users And Computers console, right-click the Mgmt1 OU and click Delegate Control. The Delegation Of Control Wizard is displayed.

7. Click Next. The *Users Or Groups* page is displayed.

8. Click Add. The Select Users, Computers, Or Groups dialog box is displayed.

9. Key **Manager** in the Enter The Object Names To Select text box, and then click Check Names. The Manager username should now appear underlined. Click OK.

10. In the *Users Or Groups* page, click Next. The *Tasks To Delegate* page is displayed.

11. Place a checkmark next to Reset User Passwords and Force Password Change At Next Logon. Click Next, and then click Finish.

12. Move the User1 account from the Users container to the Mgmt1 OU. You can use the drag-and-drop method to move the user account. You can also right-click the user account and then click Move. A Move dialog box is displayed. Select the Mgmt1 OU, and then click OK.

13. Open a command-prompt window. Key the following command and then press Enter:

    - **dsmove cn=user2,cn=users,dc=domain*xx*,dc=local –newparent ou=Mgmt1,dc=domain*xx*,dc=local**

14. In the left pane of the Active Directory Users And Computers console, select the Mgmt1 OU. Refresh the display by clicking Refresh on the Action menu or by pressing F5. User1 and User2 should be displayed in the right pane.

15. Close the command-prompt window, close the Active Directory Users And Computers console, and log off of the computer.

■ PART B: Delegating Control on the Child Domain

1. On the even-numbered computer, log on as the default administrator of the childyy domain.

2. Open a command prompt window and key the following three commands to create user accounts that you will delegate limited permissions to:

    - **dsadd user cn=User3,cn=Users,dc=child*yy*,dc=domain*xx*,dc=local –samid User3 –upn user3@child*yy*.domain*xx*.local –pwd MSPress#1**

    - **dsadd user cn=User4,cn=Users,dc=child*yy*,dc=domain*xx*,dc=local –samid User4 –upn user4@child*yy*.domain*xx*.local –pwd MSPress#1**

    - **dsadd user cn=Manager,cn=Users,dc=child*yy*,dc=domain*xx*,dc=local –samid Manager –upn manager@child*yy*.domain*xx*.local –pwd MSPress#1**

3. Open the Active Directory Users And Computers console.

4. Right-click the childyy.domainxx.local object in the left pane. Click New, and then click Organizational Unit. A New Object–Organizational Unit dialog box is displayed.

5. Key **Mgmt2** in the Name text box, and then click OK.

6. In the left pane of the Active Directory Users And Computers console, right-click the Mgmt2 OU and click Delegate Control. The Delegation Of Control Wizard is displayed.

7. Click Next. The *Users Or Groups* page is displayed.

8. Click Add. The Select Users, Computers, Or Groups dialog box is displayed.

9. Key **Manager** in the Enter The Object Names To Select text box, and then click Check Names. The Manager username should now appear underlined. Click OK.

10. In the *Users Or Groups* page, click Next. The *Tasks To Delegate* page is displayed.

11. Select Reset User Passwords and Force Password Change At Next Logon. Click Next, and then click Finish.

12. Move the User3 account from the Users container to the Mgmt2 OU. You can use the drag-and-drop method to move the user account. You can also right-click the user account and then click Move. A Move dialog box is displayed. Select the Mgmt2 OU, and then click OK.

13. Open a command prompt window. Key the following command and then press Enter:

    - **dsmove cn=user4,cn=users,dc=childyy,dc=domainxx,dc=local –newparent ou=Mgmt2,dc=childyy,dc=domainxx,dc=local**

14. In the left pane of the Active Directory Users And Computers console, select the Mgmt2 OU. Refresh the display by clicking Refresh on the Action menu or by pressing F5. User3 and User4 should appear in the right pane.

15. Close the command-prompt window, close the Active Directory Users And Computers console, and log off of the computer.

■ PART C: Testing Delegated Permissions on the Parent Domain

1. On the odd-numbered computer, log on using the Manager user account in the domain*xx* domain. The password is MSPress#1 or the password that was assigned to you by your instructor or lab proctor.

2. Open the Active Directory Users And Computers console. When prompted, reenter the password for the Manager account to continue.

3. In the left window pane, expand the domain*xx*.local object and click the Mgmt1 OU.

4. In the right pane, right-click User2 and click Reset Password. The Reset Password dialog box is displayed.

5. Key **MSPress#1** or the password that has been assigned to you in the New Password text box and in the Confirm Password text box. Click OK. The Active Directory message box is displayed, verifying that the user's password has changed. Click OK.

6. In the right window pane, right-click User1 and click Delete.

7. An Active Directory warning message is displayed asking you to confirm the deletion of the account. Click Yes.

8. The Active Dirctory message box is displayed, telling you that you do not have sufficient privileges to delete the user account. Click OK.

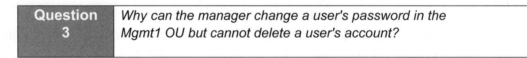

Question 3	*Why can the manager change a user's password in the Mgmt1 OU but cannot delete a user's account?*

9. Try changing the password for another user that is not a member of the Mgmt1 OU; for example, the Administrator in the Users container.

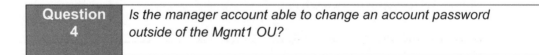

Question 4	*Is the manager account able to change an account password outside of the Mgmt1 OU?*

10. Close the Active Directory Users And Computers console and log off of the computer.

■ PART D: Testing Delegated Permissions on the Child Domain

1. On the even-numbered computer, log on using the Manager user account in the child*yy* domain. The password is MSPress#1 or the password that was assigned to you by your instructor or lab proctor.

2. Open the Active Directory Users And Computers console. When prompted, reenter the password for the Manager account to continue.

3. In the left window pane, expand the domain*xx*.local object and click the Mgmt2 OU.

4. In the right pane, right-click User3 and click Reset Password. The Reset Password dialog box is displayed.

5. Key **MSPress#1** or the password that has been assigned to you in the New Password text box and in the Confirm Password text box. Click OK. The Active Directory message box is displayed, verifying that the user's password has changed. Click OK.

6. In the right window pane, right-click User3 and click Delete.

7. An Active Directory warning message is displayed asking you to confirm the deletion of the account. Click Yes.

8. The Active Dirctory message box is displayed, telling you that you do not have sufficient privileges to delete the user account. Click OK.

Question 5	*Why can the manager change a user's password in the Mgmt2 OU but cannot delete a user's account?*

9. Try changing the password for another user that is not a member of the Mgmt2 OU; for example, the Administrator in the Users container.

Question 6	*Is the manager account able to change an account password outside of the Mgmt2 OU?*

10. Close the Active Directory Users And Computers console and log off of the computer.

LAB REVIEW QUESTIONS

Completion time	15 minutes

1. In your own words, describe what you learned by completing this lab.

2. If you delegate administrative control over an OU to allow password changes, should that user be able to delete user accounts within the OU?

3. True or False? You should not be able to open more than two administrative consoles with the runas command.

LAB CHALLENGE 6.1	USING DSMOVE
Overview	Your manager tells you to create three top-level OUs: Acct, AcctPay, and AcctRec. After you do this, your manager tells you to move the AcctRec and AcctPay OUs so that they are child OUs of the Acct OU. You decide to accomplish this using the dsmove program.
Outcomes	After completing this exercise, you will know how to: • Create an OU. • Use dsmove to modify an OU.
Completion time	5 minutes
Precautions	N/A

Task 1: Create the three top-level OUs in your domain. Name them AcctRec, AcctPay, and Acct. Use dsmove to make the AcctRec and AcctPay OUs subordinate to the Acct OU.

LAB CHALLENGE 6.2	MOVING OBJECTS WITH ADMT
Overview	Your manager tells you that several objects in the parent Active Directory domain need to be moved into a child domain that was recently added to your company's Active Directory infrastructure. Your manager wants to know if the user's Security Identifier (SID) will change if any user accounts need to be moved.
Outcomes	Use ADMT to move Active Directory objects.
Completion time	20 minutes
Precautions	N/A

Task 1: Check the SID of the domainxx\User1 and domainxx\User2 user accounts using whoami /all.

Task 2: Using ADMT, move the Mgmt1 OU and the user objects it contains from the parent domain to the child domain. Ask your instructor for the location of the ADMT or download it from the Microsoft Website. (Hint: You must be logged on as a user account with domain admin privileges in both domains to accomplish this task.)

Task 3: Use whoami /all to determine if the SIDs of the User1 and User2 accounts are different after they have been moved into a new domain.

LAB 7
EXPLORING GROUP POLICY ADMINISTRATION

This lab contains the following projects and activities:

Project 7.1   Configuring the Local Computer Policy

Project 7.2   Configuring Processing Order

Project 7.3   Configuring Priority Order

Project 7.4   Using Block Policy Inheritance and Enforce

Project 7.5   Using Group Policy Loopback Processing

Lab Review Questions

Lab Challenge 7.1   Disabling the Shutdown Event Tracker

Lab Challenge 7.2   Hiding Last Logged-on Username

Post-Lab Cleanup

BEFORE YOU BEGIN

Lab 7 assumes that you completed the setup process as specified in the setup document and that your computer has connectivity to other lab computers and the Internet. Lab 7 also assumes that you have completed the nonoptional exercises in the previous labs. Specifically, Lab 7 assumes the following:

- The even-numbered computer (RWDC*yy*) must be configured to use the odd-numbered computer (RWDC*xx*) as its preferred DNS server, as explained in Lab 1, Project 1.4.
- Active Directory is installed on the odd-numbered computer (RWDC*xx*), as described in Lab 2, Project 2.1 and Project 2.2.
- Active Directory is installed on the even-numbered computer (RWDC*yy*), as described in Lab 2, Project 2.5.
- Users have the right to log on to domain controllers, as described in Lab 5, Project 5.1.

In this lab, you will see the characters xx, yy, and zz. These directions assume that students are working in pairs, and that each student has a number. One number is odd and the other number is even. For example, the first student pair will consist of RWDC01 as the first odd-numbered computer and RWDC02 as the first even-numbered computer, RWDC03 and RWDC04 as the second student pair, and RWDC05 and RWDC06 as the third student pair. When you see "xx" in this manual, substitute the unique number assigned to the odd-numbered computer in a pair. When you see "yy", substitute the unique number assigned to the even-numbered computer in a pair. **When you see "zz", substitute the number assigned to the computer that you are currently working at, regardless of whether it is odd or even.**

SCENARIO

You are the network administrator of Lucerne Publishing. Lucerne Publishing has offices worldwide. The company has a single Active Directory domain named lucernepublishing.com. The company has 12 locations in 12 different countries: Australia, Egypt, Nigeria, Saudi Arabia, Luxembourg, France, Indonesia, Greece, Germany, Italy, the Netherlands, and the United States.

The company network has 15 domain controllers. All of the domain controllers run Microsoft Windows Server 2008, Enterprise Edition. Three domain controllers are located at the company headquarters in Tempe, Arizona. The rest of the domain controllers are distributed evenly, one per country, to the company's other locations.

You are employed by the company's U.S. location and work in the Tempe, Arizona, office. Tempe is considered the company headquarters, and its network is associated with the American_Site Active Directory site. The other site names are as follows: Au_Site, Egyptian_Site, Nigerian_Site, Saudi_Site, Lux_Site, French_Site, Indo_Site, Greek_Site, German_Site, Italian_Site, and Dutch_Site.

Each country's user and computer accounts are configured in an OU named after the city in which the users and computers are located. The OU names are as follows: Tempe, Melbourne, Cairo, Calabar, Saudi City, Lux City, Paris, Java, Santorini, Berlin, Florence, and Baarn.

You are assigned the task of standardizing the desktops for users across the enterprise. As you gather information about the needs of each location, you realize that you must consider the locale differences and exactly how Group Policy flows through the domain. You decide to configure your test lab as a single domain with one client, a member server. Then you decide that you must test the following:

- Domain policy and local computer policy interaction
- Multiple policies and the priority of their application
- Block Policy Inheritance versus Enforce
- Loopback Processing Mode

After completing this lab, you will be able to:

■ Explain how policy inheritance affects the application of Group Policy settings.

■ Configure some Group Policy Objects (GPOs) to have a higher priority than other GPOs.

■ Configure OUs with Block Policy Inheritance.

■ Enable the Enforce setting on GPO links.

■ Configure Loopback Processing Mode.

Estimated lesson time: 170 minutes

Project 7.1	Configuring the Local Computer Policy
Overview	You need to prepare your test lab for your upcoming experiments. First, remove a child domain that you have configured. Then, configure a member server as a member of the remaining forest root domain. Finally, test the implementation of a Local GPO before you move on to testing Group Policy Objects (GPOs.)
Outcomes	After completing this exercise, you will know how to: • Demote a domain controller to member server status. • View and configure the local computer policy.
Completion time	35 minutes
Precautions	Both parts of this exercise should only be performed on the even-numbered computers. If you have completed the optional exercises in Lab 2, follow all of the steps in this lab. If you skipped the optional exercises, begin with step 7 of Part A.

■ PART A: Removing the Child Domain

1. Press Ctrl+Alt+Delete on the SCDC*yy* computer and log on as the default domain administrator of the child*yy* domain. Your username will be Administrator. The password will be MSPress#1 or the password that your instructor or lab proctor has assigned to you. Using Notepad, create a file called *c:\demote.txt* containing the following information:

    [DCINSTALL]
    UserName=administrator@child*yy*.domain*xx*.local
    Password=MSPress#1
    UserDomain=child*yy*.domain*xx*.local
    AdministratorPassword=MSPress#1
    IsLastDCInDomain=No
    RebootOnSuccess=Yes

2. Open a command-prompt window and key **dcpromo /answer:"c:\demote.txt"**. Press Enter. After the Server Core domain controller is demoted, it will reboot automatically. Log on to the Server Core computer as the local administrator and power down the server, because it is not required for the remainder of this lab.

3. Press Ctrl+Alt+Delete on the RODC*yy* computer and log on as the default domain administrator of the child*yy* domain. Your username will be Administrator. The password will be MSPress#1 or the password that your instructor or lab proctor has assigned to you. Close the Server Manager window if it appears automatically. Using Notepad, create a file called *c:\demote.txt* containing the following information:

[DCINSTALL]
UserName=administrator@child*yy*.domain*xx*.local
Password=MSPress#1
UserDomain=child*yy*.domain*xx*.local
AdministratorPassword=MSPress#1
IsLastDCInDomain=No
RebootOnCompletion=Yes

4.   Open a command-prompt window and key **dcpromo /answer:"c:\demote.txt"**. Press Enter. After the domain controller is demoted, it will reboot automatically. Log on to the server as the local administrator and power down the server, because it is not required for the remainder of this lab.

5.   Press Ctrl+Alt+Delete on the RWDC*yy* computer and log on as the default domain administrator of the child*yy* domain. Your username will be Administrator. The password will be MSPress#1 or the password that your instructor or lab proctor has assigned to you. Using Notepad, create a file called *c:\demote.txt* containing the following information:

[DCINSTALL]
UserName=administrator@ domain*xx*.local
Password=MSPress#1
UserDomain= domain*xx*.local
AdministratorPassword=MSPress#1
RemoveApplicationPartitions=Yes
IsLastDCInDomain=Yes
RebootOnSuccess=Yes

6.   Open a command-prompt window, key **dcpromo /answer:"c:\demote.txt"**, and press Enter. After the domain controller is demoted, it will reboot automatically.

7.   Log on to the RWDC*yy* computer as the default administrator of the local computer.

8.   Open Server Manager. Browse to Computer Information and click Change System Properties. On the Computer Name tab, click Change. Click More and remove the child*yy*.domain*xx*.local primary DNS suffix.

9.   Click OK twice. The Computer Name/Domain Changes window is displayed. Read the message and click OK. Click close and restart the computer.

10.   Log on the RWDCYY computer as the default administrator of the local computer, browse to Roles Summary and click Remove Roles. Remove the Active Directory Domain Services role and the DNS Server role. Restart the even-numbered computer, if prompted to do so.

11.   Confirm that the even-numbered computer is configured to use the IP address of RWDC*xx* as its primary DNS server. Join the even-numbered computer to the domain*xx*.local domain, using the steps in Lab 2, Project 2.3.

■ PART B: Configure the Even-Numbered Computer to Remove the Properties Option When Right-Clicking My Computer

1. Log on to the even-numbered computer as the default administrator of the local computer.

2. Click the Start button. Key **gpedit.msc** and press Enter. The Group Policy Object Editor opens to the Local Computer Policy.

3. Under the User Configuration node, click Administrative Templates.

4. Click the Desktop node.

5. In the right window, double-click the Remove Properties From The Computer Icon Context Menu setting. The Remove Properties From The Computer Icon Context Menu dialog box is displayed.

6. Click the Enabled radio button, as shown in Figure 7-1. Click OK.

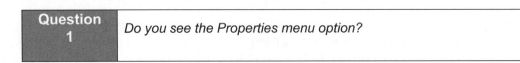

Figure 7-1
Remove Properties From The Computer Icon Context Menu

7. Close the Group Policy Management Editor.

8. Log off of the computer and then log on again as the default administrator of the local computer. This will update the Group Policy for this user account.

9. Click the Start button, and then right-click the Computer icon.

Question 1	Do you see the Properties menu option?

Project 7.2	Configuring Processing Order
Overview	The administrators in Calabar and Cairo are concerned with the potential implication of domain-wide policies. Specifically, they are concerned about domain policies overriding configured computer settings. You want to find out if they are correct.
Outcomes	After completing this exercise, you will know how to: • Create and link a domain-based Group Policy Object.
Completion time	30 minutes
Precautions	N/A

■ PART A: Configure the Computer Properties Context Menu Setting on the Domain

1. Log on to the odd-numbered computer as the default administrator of the domain*xx*.local domain.

2. Open the Group Policy Management Console from the Administrative Tools folder. Drill down to the Group Policy Objects node.

3. Right-click Default Domain Policy and click Edit. The Group Policy Management Editor window is displayed.

4. Under the User Configuration node, click Policies, and then click Administrative Templates.

5. Click the Desktop node.

6. In the right window, double-click the Remove Properties From The Computer Icon Context Menu setting. The Remove Properties From The Computer Icon Context Menu dialog box is displayed.

7. Click the Disabled radio button, and then click OK.

8. Close the Group Policy Management Editor and the Group Policy Management Console.

■ PART B: Verify that the Domain GPO Overrides the Local Computer Policy

1. On the even-numbered computer, log off and then log on as the default administrator of the domain*xx*.local domain.

2. Click the Start button, and then right-click the Computer icon.

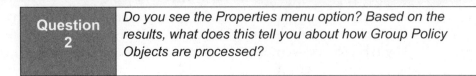

Question 2	*Do you see the Properties menu option? Based on the results, what does this tell you about how Group Policy Objects are processed?*

■ PART C: Create Domain Users for Testing

1. On the odd-numbered computer, open the Active Directory Users And Computers console.

2. Create a user account named L7DomUser in the Users container of domain*xx*.local.

3. Create a new top-level OU named L7Test1.

4. Create a user account in the L7Test1 OU named L7Test1User.

■ PART D: Create GPO Links for the Domain

1. Log on to the odd-numbered computer as the default administrator of the domain*xx*.local domain.

2. Open the Group Policy Management Console from the Administrative Tools folder. Drill down to the domain*xx* node.

3. Right-click the domain*xx* node and select Create A GPO In This Domain, And Link It Here.

4. Name the new GPO RemoveHelp1 and press Enter.

5. Navigate to the Group Policy Objects node. Right-click the RemoveHelp1 GPO and click Edit. The Group Policy Management Editor is displayed.

6. Browse to User Configuration, click Policies, and then click the Administrative Templates node.

7. Select the Start Menu and Taskbar object.

8. In the right pane, double-click the Remove Help Menu From Start Menu setting. The Remove Help Menu From Start Menu Properties dialog box is displayed.

9. Select the Enabled radio button and click OK.

10. Close the Group Policy Management Editor.

11. Right-click the domain*xx* node and select Create A GPO In This Domain, And Link It Here.

12. Name the new GPO RemoveSearch1 and press Enter.

13. Repeat steps 5–10 to enable the Remove Search Link From Start Menu setting in the RemoveSearch1 GPO. Close the Group Policy Management Editor when you are finished.

■ PART E: Create GPO Links for an OU

1. On the odd-numbered computer, open the Group Policy Management Console. Drill down to the L7Test1 OU and select Create A GPO In This Domain, And Link It Here.

2. Name the new GPO AddHelp1 and press Enter.

3. Use the technique that you used in Part D to disable the Remove Help Menu From Start Menu setting in the AddHelp1 GPO. Close the Group Policy Management Editor when you are finished.

4. Create and link another GPO to the L7Test1 OU named RemoveComputerProperties2. Enable the Remove Properties From The Computer Icon Context Menu setting in the RemoveComputerProperties2 GPO.

5. Close the Group Policy Management Editor and the Group Policy Management Console when you are finished.

■ PART F: Testing the Results

1. On the even-numbered computer, log on as L7DomUser in the domain*xx* domain.

2. Click the Start button.

Question 3	Do you see a Search menu option? Do you see a Help and Support menu option?

3. Click the Start button and right-click the Computer icon.

Question 4	Do you see the Properties context menu option?

4. Log off and then log on as L7Test1User in the domain*xx* domain.

5. Click the Start button.

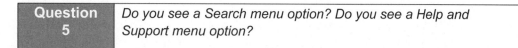

Question 5	Do you see a Search menu option? Do you see a Help and Support menu option?

6. Click the Start button and right-click the Computer icon.

Question 6	Do you see the Properties context menu option? **No**

Project 7.3	Configuring Priority Order
Overview	Administrators in Baarn tell you that they have created several child OUs. They want to know what will happen when they link two conflicting policies on the same OU.
Outcomes	After completing this exercise, you will know how to: • Test the application of multiple Group Policy Objects.
Completion time	10 minutes
Precautions	During this exercise, you will be switching back and forth between the odd- and even-numbered computers. When you switch from one computer to another, perform all steps on that computer until you are instructed to switch computers again.

■ PART A: Create an Additional GPO for L7Test1

1. On the odd-numbered computer, create a new GPO linked to the L7Test1 OU. Name it AddComputerProperties1.

2. Edit the AddComputerProperties1 GPO and disable the Remove Properties From The Computer Icon Context Menu setting.

3. On the even-numbered computer, log off and log on as L7Test1User in the domain*xx* domain.

Question 7	Can you see the Properties option when you right-click the Computer icon? Why did the AddComputerProperties1 GPO link not add this option to the Computer icon's right-click context menu?

4. On the odd-numbered computer, open the Group Policy Management Console and drill down to the L7Test1 OU.

5. Click the AddComputerProperties1 GPO link and then click the up arrow twice. Verify that the AddComputerProperties1 GPO link is at the top of the Link Order, as shown in Figure 7-2.

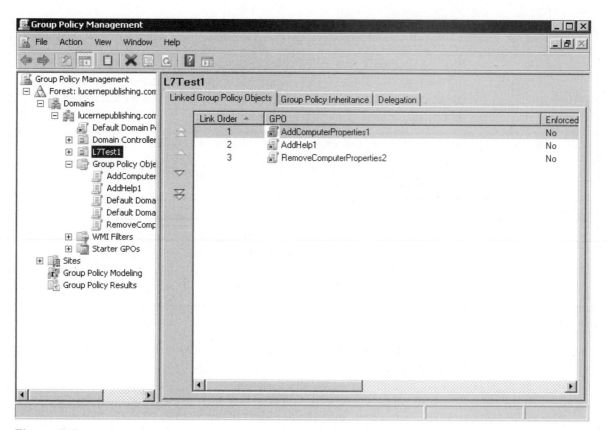

Figure 7-2
AddComputerProperties1 GPO

6. Close the Group Policy Management Console.

7. On the even-numbered computer, open a command-prompt window.

8. Key **gpupdate /force** and press Enter.

9. Click the Start button, and then right-click the Computer icon.

Question 8	Can you see the Properties menu option? Why did the AddComputerProperties1 GPO add this option to the Computer icon's context menu?

Project 7.4	Using Block Policy Inheritance and Enforce
Overview	It is not necessary that all GPO settings apply to all users or computers in the domain. Some users and computers do not need to receive some of the configuration options. You want to be able to control which settings are inherited from the domain by specific OUs.
Outcomes	After completing this exercise, you will know how to: • Test the application of the Block Policy Inheritance and Enforce settings.
Completion time	25 minutes
Precautions	During this exercise, you will be switching back and forth between the odd- and even-numbered computers. When you switch from one computer to another, perform all steps on that computer until you are instructed to switch computers again.

1. On the odd-numbered computer, open the Group Policy Management Console. Drill down to the L7Test1 OU.

2. Right-click the AddComputerProperties1 GPO link and click Delete. A Group Policy Management dialog box is displayed. Read the message and click OK.

3. Right-click the AddHelp1 GPO link and click Delete. A Group Policy Management dialog box is displayed. Read the message and click OK. Right-click the RemoveComputerProperties2 GPO link and click Delete. A Group Policy Management dialog box is displayed. Read the message and click OK.

4. On the even-numbered computer, open a command-prompt window. Key **gpupdate /force** and press Enter.

5. Click the Start button.

Question 9	Do you see a Search menu option? Do you see a Help and Support menu option?

6. Click the Start button and right-click the Computer icon.

Question 10	Do you see the Properties context menu option?

7.   On the odd-numbered computer, open the Group Policy Management Console. Drill down to the L7Test1 OU.

8.   Right-click the L7Test1OU and click Block Inheritance.

9.   Click the Start button.

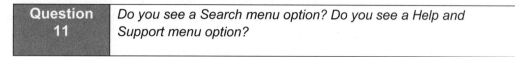

Question 11	Do you see a Search menu option? Do you see a Help and Support menu option?

10. Click the **Start** button on the even numbered computer and right-click the **Computer** icon.

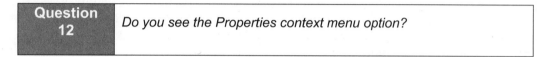

Question 12	Do you see the Properties context menu option?

11. Open the Group Policy Management Console from the Administrative Tools folder. Drill down to the domain*xx* node.

12. Right-click Default Domain Policy GPO link and click Enforced.

13. Click the Start button.

Question 13	Do you see a Search menu option? Do you see a Help and Support menu option?

14. Click the Start button and right-click the Computer icon.

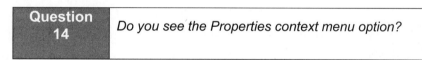

Question 14	Do you see the Properties context menu option?

Project 7.5	Using Group Policy Loopback Processing
Overview	Each top-level OU in your company has a single child OU called Employee-Access. Each of these OUs contains two computers that users visiting from other countries can use. These systems are a concern for all administrators, because administrators want visiting users to be subject to stricter controls than employees based at that location. You need to set up a method for securing these Employee-Access computers so that the desktops used by visiting users are locked down.
Outcomes	After completing this exercise, you will know how to: • Configure Group Policy Loopback Processing.
Completion time	20 minutes
Precautions	During this exercise, you will be switching back and forth between the odd- and even-numbered computers. When you switch from one computer to another, perform all steps on that computer until you are instructed to switch computers again.

1. On the odd-numbered computer, open the Active Directory Users And Computers console. Create a new top-level OU named L7Test2 in domain*xx*.local.

2. In the left pane, click the Computers container. Right-click RWDC*yy* and click Move. The Move dialog box is displayed. Select the L7Test2 OU and click OK.

3. Open the Group Policy Management Console from the Administrative Tools folder. Drill down to the L7Test2 node.

4. Right-click the L7Test2 node and select Create A GPO In This Domain, And Link It Here.

5. Name the newly created GPO DisableCP. Navigate to the Group Policy Objects node. Right-click DisableCP and click Edit. The Group Policy Management Editor is displayed.

6. Drill down to User Configuration, click Policies, click Administrative Templates, and then click Control Panel. Enable the Prohibit Access To The Control Panel setting.

7. On the even-numbered computer, log off and log on as L7DomUser of the domain*xx* domain.

8. Click the Start button and click Control Panel.

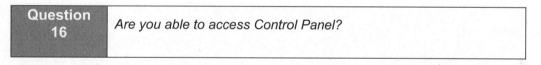

Question 15	Why are you able to access the Control Panel using L7DomUser credentials?

9. On the odd-numbered computer, edit the DisableCP GPO. Navigate to Computer Configuration, click policies, click Administrative Templates, click System, and then click Group Policy. Enable the User Group Policy Loopback Processing Mode setting. Leave the Mode drop-down box set to Replace.

10. Close the Group Policy Management Editor.

11. On the even-numbered computer, click the Start button. Key **runas /user:administrator@domain*xx*.local cmd** and press Enter. (Because User Group Policy Loopback Processing Mode is a computer setting, you need to run gpupdate as an administrator.) Key the administrator password when prompted and press Enter. When the command-prompt window is displayed, key **gpupdate /force** and press Enter.

12. On the even-numbered computer, log off and log on as L7DomUser.

13. Click the Start button.

Question 16	Are you able to access Control Panel?

LAB REVIEW QUESTIONS

Completion time	15 minutes

1. In your own words, describe what you learned by completing this lab.

2. If there is a conflict between a setting configured in the Local Computer Policy and a setting configured in a domain-linked GPO, which policy setting will be applied?

3. If multiple policies are configured at the domain level and you only want one of those policies to flow down to a given OU, what should you do to that OU? What should you do to the policy that you want to flow down?

4. You have two conflicting policies: PolicyA and PolicyB. Each is linked to the same OU named Marketing. PolicyA settings are implemented over PolicyB settings, but you need to implement PolicyB settings instead of PolicyA settings. You do not want to use No Override, because that will affect all child OUs. What should you do?

5. The Enforce setting on a GPO overrides which GPO control measure?

LAB CHALLENGE 7.1	DISABLING THE SHUTDOWN EVENT TRACKER
Overview	You want to disable the Shutdown Event Tracker so that you do not have to select a reason for turning off your test computers.
Outcomes	After completing this exercise, you will know how to: • Create, Modify, and Link a GPO. • Search for a GPO setting.
Completion time	15 minutes
Precautions	If you skip Lab Challenge 7.1, you must still complete the Post-Lab Cleanup activities before continuing to Lab 8.

Create a Group Policy named *DSET* and link the GPO to the domain. Disable the Display Shutdown Event Tracker setting.

LAB CHALLENGE 7.2	HIDING LAST LOGGED-ON USERNAME
Overview	The network administrators in Saudi Arabia do not like that the last logged on username is displayed in the Windows dialog box. They do not want network users to be able to find out other users' usernames so easily.
Outcomes	After completing this exercise, you will know how to: • Create, modify, and link a GPO. • Search for a GPO setting.
Completion time	5 minutes
Precautions	If you skip Lab Challenge 7.2, you must still complete the Post-Lab Cleanup activities before continuing to Lab 8.

Create a Group Policy Object named ClearName1 and link the GPO to the domain. Enable the Interactive Logon: Do Not Display Last User Name setting.

POST-LAB CLEANUP	
Overview	The following cleanup activities must be performed before moving on to Lab 8.
Completion time	5 minutes

1. Permanently delete all new GPO objects that you created in this Lab as follows:

   • Open the Group Policy Management Console.

   • Navigate to the Group Policy Objects node.

   • Right-click the GPO and click Delete. A Group Policy Management dialog box will be displayed. Click Yes to delete the GPO.

> **NOTE** *Do not delete the Default Domain Policy or the Default Domain Controllers Policy.*

2. Move the RWDC*yy* computer account from the L7Test2 OU to the Computers container.

3. Open the Active Directory Users and Computers snap-in. Click View, and then click Advanced Features.

4. Right-click the L7Test1 OU and select Properties. Click the Object tab. Remove the checkmark next to Protect Object From Accidental Deletion. Click OK.

5. Right-click the L7Test1 OU and click Delete. Click Yes to confirm the deletion. The Confirm Subtree Deletion message box is displayed. Click Yes.

6. Right-click the L7Test2 OU and select Properties. Click the Object tab. Remove the checkmark next to Protect Object From Accidental Deletion. Click OK.

7. Right-click the L7Test2 OU and click Delete. Click Yes to confirm the deletion. A Confirm Subtree Deletion message box is displayed. Click Yes.

8. Edit the Default Domain Policy and set the Remove Properties from the Computer icon context menu setting to Not Configured.

9. Navigate to the domain*xx*.local node. Right-click the Default Domain Policy GPO link and remove the checkmark next to No Override.

10. On the even-numbered computer, edit the Local Computer Policy and change the Remove Properties From The Computer Icon Context Menu setting to Not Configured.

11. Execute **gpupdate /force** on the odd- and even-numbered computers.

12. Log off of each computer and log back on as the default administrator in the domain*xx* domain. Verify that the Help, Support, and Search options are available on the Start Menu. Verify that you can open the Control Panel and that the Properties option is displayed when you right-click the Computer icon in the Start Menu. If not, try restarting the servers or verifying the Post-Lab Cleanup steps.

LAB 8
MANAGING USERS AND COMPUTERS WITH GROUP POLICY

This lab contains the following projects and activities:

Project 8.1 Configuring Account Policies

Project 8.2 Configuring Audit Policies

Project 8.3 Configuring Folder Redirection

Project 8.4 Enabling Disk Quotas

Lab Review Questions

Lab Challenge 8.1 Configure a Fine-Grained Password Policy

Post-Lab Cleanup

BEFORE YOU BEGIN

Lab 8 assumes that setup has been completed as specified in the setup document, and that your computer has connectivity to other lab computers and the Internet. Lab 8 also assumes that you have completed the non-optional exercises in the previous labs. Specifically, Lab 8 assumes the following:

- The even-numbered computer (RWDC*yy*) must be configured to use the odd-numbered computer (RWDC*xx*) as its preferred DNS server, as described in Lab 1, Project 1.4.
- Active Directory is installed on the odd-numbered computer (RWDC*xx*), as described in Lab 2, Project 2.1 and Project 2.2.
- The even-numbered computer is configured as a member server in the domain*xx*.local domain, as described in Lab 7, Project 7.1.
- Users have the right to log on to domain controllers, as described in Lab 5, Project 5.1.

NOTE	*In this lab, you will see the characters xx, yy, and zz. These directions assume that students are working in pairs, and that each student has a number. One number is odd and the other number is even. For example, the first student pair will consist of RWDC01 as the first odd-numbered computer and RWDC02 as the first even-numbered computer, RWDC03 and RWDC04 as the second student pair, and RWDC05 and RWDC06 as the third student pair. When you see "xx" in this manual, substitute the unique number assigned to the odd-numbered computer in a pair. When you see "yy", substitute the unique number assigned to the even-numbered computer in a pair. **When you see "zz", substitute the number assigned to the computer that you are currently working at, regardless of whether it is odd or even.***

SCENARIO

You are a network administrator for Fabrikam. Fabrikam uses a single Active Directory domain. The Fabrikam network has three Windows Server 2008 domain controllers and 500 client computers running Windows XP Professional.

Recently, a security consulting company conducted an analysis of the Fabrikam network. Your manager wants you to address the following issues:

- Password-cracking software was run on the network, but the target accounts were never locked out as a result of incorrect logon attempts.

- Files identified by management as being confidential are not being monitored.

- Some users have set passwords that are shorter than the stated Fabrikam corporate standard.

Your manager wants you to back up the My Documents folder for every Marketing Department user each day. You are concerned that this may lead to a shortage of disk space on the server. You also want to ensure that users' disk space is limited on any file server used to save the files.

After completing this lab, you will be able to:

- Enforce a password policy.

- Administer an Account Lockout policy.

- Configure security auditing.

- Redirect users' folders to a central location.

- Enable centralized disk quotas.

Estimated lesson time: 150 minutes

Project 8.1	Configuring Account Policies
Overview	Some departments in your company require a 14-character password for user accounts. You want to ensure that users are required to use 14-character passwords. Furthermore, you need to address the issue that the security consultants identified concerning account lockout. The security consultants were able to run a password cracker on your network without locking out a single user account. You want to ensure that anyone attempting to gain access to a user account by trying different passwords is locked out.
Outcomes	After completing this exercise, you will know how to: • Configure a domain-wide password policy. • Configure a domain-wide account lockout policy.
Completion time	20 minutes
Precautions	During this exercise, you will be switching back and forth between the odd- and even-numbered computers. When you switch from one computer to another, it is important that you remain on that computer for the steps that follow until you are instructed to switch again.

■ PART A: Adjusting a Local Password Policy

1. On the odd-numbered computer, log on as the default administrator of the domain*xx*.local domain.

2. Create an OU named Marketing.

3. Create and link a new GPO to the Marketing OU named PwdPol1. Right-click the PwdPol1 GPO and click Edit.

4. Browse to Computer Configuration, click Policies, click Windows Settings, click Security Settings, click Account Policies, and then click Password Policy.

5. Double-click Minimum Password Length. The Minimum Password Length Properties dialog box will be displayed.

6. Place a checkmark next to Define This Policy Setting. Configure the minimum password length to Password Must Be At Least 14 Characters, and then click OK.

7. Close the Group Policy Management Editor.

8. Create a user named *Lab8User1* in the Marketing OU with a password of MSPress#1 and clear the User Must Change Password At Next Logon checkbox.

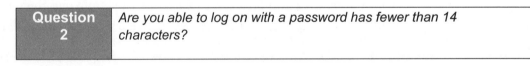

Question 1	*MSPress#1 is a nine-character password. Why are you not required to use a 14-character password?*

9. In the Group Policy Management snap-in, right-click the domain*xx*.local node and select Link An Existing GPO. The Select GPO window is displayed. Click PwdPol1 and click OK.

10. On the Linked Group Policy Objects tab, select the GPO link to PwdPol1. Click the Up arrow until the link to PwdPol1 is first in the Link Order.

11. Remove the GPO link to PwdPol1 from the Marketing OU.

12. Configure Block Policy Inheritance for the Marketing OU. Refer to Lab 7, Project 7.4, if necessary.

13. On the even-numbered computer, log on as Lab8User1 on the domain*xx*.local domain.

Question 2	*Are you able to log on with a password has fewer than 14 characters?*

14. Open a command-prompt window, key **gpupdate /force** and press Enter.

15. On the odd-numbered computer, create a user account in the Markteing OU named Lab8User2 and try to configure the password as MSPress#1. An Active Directory message box is displayed. Read the message and click OK.

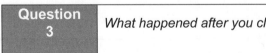

Question 3	*What happened after you clicked OK?*

16. Click Back. Key **MSPress#1MSPress#1** into the Password text box and the Confirm Password text box.

17. Click Next and then click Finish.

 Does this password work? What does this teach you about password policy inheritance?

■ PART B: Adjusting the Account Lockout Policy

1. Use the technique you learned in the previous section to edit the PwdPol1 GPO. Click Computer Configuration, click Policies, click Windows Settings, click Security Settings, click Account Policies, click Account Lockout Policy. Configure the Account Lockout Threshold setting for three Invalid Logon Attempts. When you click OK to configure this setting, a Suggested Value Changes message box is displayed. Click OK.

2. Close the Group Policy Management Editor.

3. On the even-numbered computer, log off and attempt to log on with the Lab8User1 credentials, but when providing the password credentials use the password MSP. Repeat this process three more times.

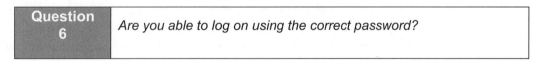 *What happens to the Lab8User1 account?*

4. Attempt to log on using the correct password of MSPress#1.

Question 6 *Are you able to log on using the correct password?*

5. On the odd-numbered computer, unlock the user account. Open the Active Directory Users And Computers console and drill down to the Marketing OU in the left pane. Right-click Lab8User1 and click Properties. The Lab8User1 Properties dialog box is displayed. Click the Account tab and then clear the Account Is Locked Out checkbox. Click OK.

6. On the even-numbered computer, verify that you can log on as Lab8User1 with a password of MSPress#1. Log off.

Project 8.2	Configuring Audit Policies
Overview	The security consultants found that confidential files were not monitored for hacking attempts. You want to configure auditing of all confidential files.
Outcomes	After completing this exercise, you will know how to: • Configure auditing of the Windows file system.
Completion time	30 minutes
Precautions	This exercise will be performed on both computers. When you perform this exercise on the odd-numbered computer, you will be working with the Group Policy Management MMC snap-in. When you perform this exercise on the even-numbered computer, you will be working with the local group policy by opening the Group Policy Object Editor on the even-numbered computer.

1. Log onto RWDC*zz* as the default administrator of the domain*xx*.local domain.

2. Create a new folder called ConfidentialFiles in the root of the C:\ drive.

3. Right-click the ConfidentialFiles folder and select Properties. The ConfidentialFiles Properties dialog box is displayed.

4. Click the Security tab, and then click Advanced. The Advanced Security Settings for ConfidentialFiles dialog box is displayed.

5. Click the Auditing tab, click Edit, and then click Add. The Select User, Computer Or Group dialog box is displayed.

6. Key **Everyone** into the Enter Object Name To Select text box and click Check Names. Verify that the Everyone group is underlined and then click OK. The Auditing Entry For ConfidentialFiles dialog box is displayed.

7. In the Access box, place a checkmark next to List Folder/Read Data in the Successful and Failed columns as shown in Figure 8-1.

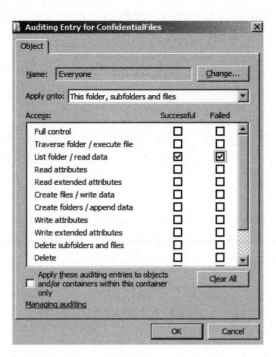

Figure 8-1
Auditing Entry for ConfidentialFiles window

8. Click OK.

9. Click OK in the Advanced Security Settings For ConfidentialFiles dialog box.

10. Create two text files in the ConfidentialFiles folder. Name one file Confidential1.txt and the other Confidential2.txt. Key **Lab8 auditing test** in each file.

11. Open the Event Viewer from the Administrative Tools folder. Select the Security log in the left pane under Windows Logs.

12. Scroll down in the right details pane. You should not see any audit events recorded here for the files that you just modified, because Audit Object Access is not enabled.

13. If you are performing this exercise on the odd-numbered computer, create a new GPO called *Audit1* and link it to the Domain Controllers OU. If you are performing this exercise on the even-numbered computer, modify the Local Security Policy directly.

14. Edit the Audit1 GPO (on the odd-numbered computer) or the Local Computer Policy (on the even-numbered computer). Browse to Computer Configuration, click Policies, click Windows Settings, click Security Settings, click Local Policies, and click Audit Policy.

15. In the right pane, double-click the Audit Object Access setting. The Audit Object Access Properties box is displayed.

16. On the odd-numbered computer, place a checkmark next to Define These Policy Settings. On both computers, place a checkmark next to Success and Failure. Click OK.

17. Close the Group Policy Management Editor on the odd-numbered computer and the Group Policy Object Editor on the even-numbered computer.

18. Close all open windows, log off, and log on as Lab8User1 on the domain*xx* domain.

19. Open the folder named ConfidentialFiles, open the file named Confidential1.txt, and then close the file.

20. Log off and log on as Lab8User2 on the domain*xx* domain using the password MSPress#1MSPress#1.

21. Open the ConfidentialFiles folder, open the Confidential2.txt file, and then close the file.

22. Use the runas command to open the Event Viewer by keying **runas /user:administrator@domain*xx*.local "mmc eventvwr.msc"** and pressing Enter. Enter the password for the administrator account and press Enter.

23. Select the Security log in the left pane.

24. In the right pane, double-click any Object Access events from Lab8User1 or Lab8User2 that have Event ID 4686, 4658, or 4663.

25. Close all open windows and log off.

Project 8.3	Configuring Folder Redirection
Overview	Many of the production users in your company have important files stored in their My Documents folders. You want to redirect all of the mobile users' documents to a central location to facilitate backup.
Outcomes	After completing this exercise, you will know how to: • Configure folder redirection.
Completion time	15 minutes
Precautions	During this exercise, you will be switching back and forth between the odd- and even-numbered computers. When you switch from one computer to another, it is important that you remain on that computer for the steps that follow until you are instructed to switch again.

1. On the odd-numbered computer, log on as the default administrator of the domain*xx*.local domain.

2. Create a folder named Lab8MyDocs1 on the C:\ drive.

3. Share the Lab8MyDocs1 folder. Configure the Everyone user as a co-owner of this share. Give the Everyone user Full Control on the share Lab8MyDocs1.

4. Create a new GPO named Redirect1 and link it to the Marketing OU.

5. Right-click the Redirect1 GPO and click Edit. Browse to User Configuration, click Policies, click Window Settings, and then click Folder Redirection.

6. Right-click Documents and select Properties. The Documents Properties dialog box is displayed.

7. In the Setting selection box, select Basic.

8. Ensure that the Target Folder Location is Create A Folder For Each User Under The Root Path. Key **\\RWDC*xx*\Lab8MyDocs1** in the Root Path text box.

9. Click OK. A warning message is displayed. Read the warning and click Yes to continue.

10. Close all open windows.

11. On the even-numbered computer, log on as Lab8User1 in the domain*xx*.local domain.

12. On the odd-numbered computer, open the Lab8MyDocs1 folder.

Question 7	*Do you see a folder named Lab8User1?*

13. Open the Lab8User1 folder.

Question 8	*Is the Documents folder for Lab8User1 redirected?*

14. Log off of the even-numbered computer

Project 8.4	**Enabling Disk Quotas**
Overview	You are concerned that users are saving too much data to the servers on your network. You want to enable disk quotas as a possible solution for the problem.
Outcomes	After completing this exercise, you will know how to: • Enable disk quotas.
Completion time	30 minutes
Precautions	N/A

1. On the odd-numbered computer, create and link a new GPO named DiskQuota1 to the domain*xx*.local domain.

2. Open the Group Policy Management Editor for the DiskQuota1 GPO and browse to Computer Configuration, click Policies, click Administrative Templates, click System, and then click Disk Quotas.

3. In the right pane, double-click Enable Disk Quotas. The Enable Disk Quotas Properties dialog box is displayed.

4. Select the Enabled radio button and click OK.

5. In the right pane, double-click Default Quota Limit And Warning. The Default Quota Limit And Warning Level Properties dialog box is displayed.

6. Select the Enabled radio button.

7.   Set the Default Quota Limit Value box to 1. Ensure that the Units box remains set to MB.

8.   Set the Default Warning Level Value to 512KB.

9.   Click Next Setting. The Log Event When Quota Limit Exceeded Properties dialog box is displayed.

10. Select the Enabled radio button. Click Next Setting. The Log Event When Quota Warning Level Exceeded Properties dialog box is displayed.

11. Select the Enabled radio button. Click OK and close the Group Policy Management Editor and the Group Policy Management MMC snap-in.

12. Create a new user account named Lab8User3 in the Marketing OU. Set the password to MSPress#1MSPress#1 and clear the User Must Change Password At Next Logon checkbox.

13. Run gpupdate /force on both computers. When prompted to restart the computer, click Y and press Enter.

14. On the even-numbered computer, log on as Lab8User3 in the domain*xx*.local domain.

15. Create a new bitmap image. Right-click the Desktop in an area without any icons, click New, and then click Bitmap image.

16. Key **Lab8Test.bmp** and then press Enter to rename the file.

17. Press the Print Screen key to take a screen capture of your Desktop.

18. Double-cick the Lab8Test.bmp file that you created in Steps 15 and 16. By default the file is opened with Paint, a Windows accessory program. (If you have modified any default settings on the Windows Server 2008 computer, a different graphics application might be used to open the file.)

19. Select the Paste comand and then save the file.

20. Use the runas command to open the Event Viewer by keying **runas /user:administrator@domain*xx*.local "mmc eventvwr.msc"** and pressing Enter. Key the password for the administrator account and press Enter.

21. Select the System log in the left pane. In the right pane, look for an Event ID of 37 from Lab8User3. When you find one, double-click it.

22. Close all open windows and log off.

LAB REVIEW QUESTIONS

Completion time	15 minutes

1. In your own words, describe what you learned during this lab.

2. When you create a GPO to implement a new password policy, where must you link the GPO to have the policy affect Active Directory domain accounts?

3. If you want to configure auditing on domain controllers, where must you create and link a GPO or modify an existing GPO?

4. Which items can you redirect under Folder Redirection in Group Policy?

5. If you configure the Reset Account Lockout Counter After setting to 0, what does this mean?

LAB CHALLENGE 8.1	CONFIGURE A FINE-GRAINED PASSWORD POLICY
Overview	Management has decided that the 14-character domain-wide password policy is too stringent and should be reduced to 8 characters. However, all members of the Domain*xx*.local\Domain Admins group need to have a 14-character password.
Outcomes	After completing this exercise, you will know how to: • Modify a domain-wide password policy. • Configure a Fine-Grained Password policy.
Completion time	20 minutes
Precautions	If you skip Lab Challenge 8.1, you must complete the Post-Lab Cleanup activities before continuing to Lab B.

This challenge involves two tasks:

• Modify the domain-wide password policy so that the minimum password length requirement is 8 characters rather than 14.

• Use ADSIEdit to create a passwordSettingsObject that is linked to the Domain Admins group with the settings identified in Table 8-1.

Table 8-1
Settings

Policy	Policy Setting
Enforce Password History	10 passwords remembered
Maximum Password Age	42 days (Hint: The value you will need to enter in ADSI Edit is -36288000000000.)
Minimum Password Age	0 days
Password Must Meet Complexity Requirements	Enabled
Store Passwords Using Reversible Encryption	Disabled
Precedence	50

POST-LAB CLEANUP

Overview	The following cleanup activities must be performed before moving on to Lab B.
Completion time	15 minutes

1. On the even-numbered computer, open the Local Computer Policy by running gpedit.msc. Navigate to Computer Configuration, click Policies, click Windows Settings, click Security Settings, click Local Policies, and then click Audit Policy. Set the Audit Object Access setting to No Auditing by clearing the Success and Failure checkboxes.

2. On the odd-numbered computer, edit the DiskQuota1 GPO linked to the domain*xx*.local domain. Browse to Computer Configuration, click Policies, click Administrative Templates, click Sysetm, and then click Disk Quotas. In the right pane, double-click Enable Disk Quotas. The Enable Disk Quotas Properties dialog box is displayed.

3. Select the Disabled radio button and click OK.

4. In the right pane, double-click Default Quota Limit And Warning. Select the Disabled radio button and click OK.

5. Click Next Setting. The Log Event When Quota Limit Exceeded Properties dialog box is displayed.

6. Select the Disabled radio button. Click Next Setting. The Log Event When Quota Warning Level Exceeded Properties dialog box is displayed.

7. Select the Disabled radio button and click OK.

8. Close the Group Policy Management Editor and the Group Policy Management MMC snap-in.

9. On both computers, go to a command-prompt window and key **gpupdate /force**.

10. On the odd-numbered computer, log on as the default administrator of the domain*xx*.local domain.

11. Permanently remove all GPOs that you created in this lab. In the domain*xx*.local domain, this includes PwdPol1, DiskQuota1, and any GPOs created in the Lab Challenges. In the Marketing OU, this includes Redirect1.

12. Delete the Marketing OU and the user objects it contains.

LAB B
TROUBLESHOOTING

BEFORE YOU BEGIN

Troubleshooting Lab B is a practical application of the knowledge you have acquired from Lessons 5 through 8 to solve problems. Troubleshooting Lab B is divided into two sections: "Reviewing a Network" and "Troubleshooting a Break Scenario." In the "Reviewing a Network" section, you will review and assess a Windows Server 2008 Active Directory network for Contoso Pharmaceuticals. In the "Troubleshooting a Break Scenario" section, you will troubleshoot a particular break scenario. In this section, your instructor or lab assistant has changed your computer configuration, causing it to "break." Your task in this section will be to apply your acquired skills to troubleshoot and resolve the break.

REVIEWING A NETWORK

In this portion of Troubleshooting Lab B, you are the network administrator for Contoso Pharmaceuticals. The company network uses a single Active Directory domain named contoso.com. The company has operations in the United States, Canada, and Mexico. A single Active Directory site represents each of these operations. The sites are named US_site, Can_site, and Mex_site.

The company has seven domain controllers running Windows Server 2008, Enterprise Edition; 15 member servers running Windows Server 2008, Standard Edition; and 500 client computers running Windows XP Professional. The domain functional level is Windows Server 2008. The Contoso Pharmaceuticals domain and OU structure is shown in Figure B-1.

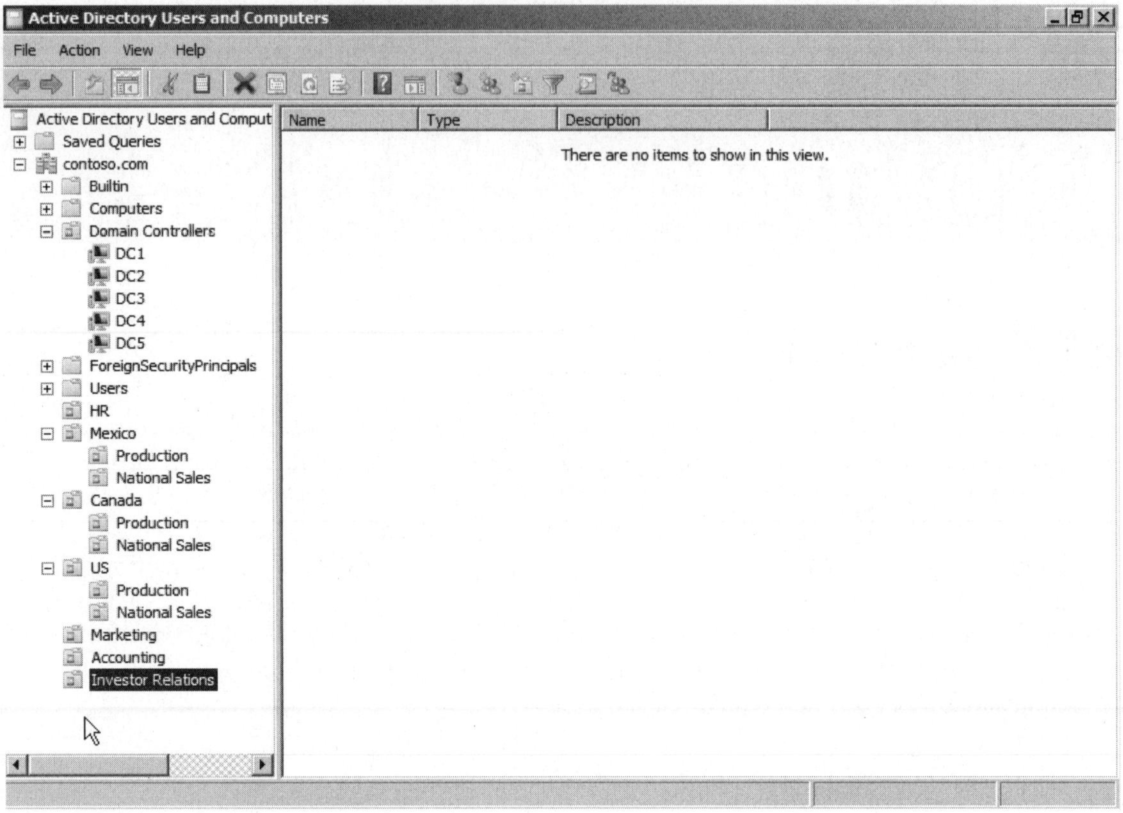

Figure B-1
Contoso Pharmaceuticals domain and OU structure

You are assigned the task of creating the administrative structure for a new location in Singapore. You must implement smart cards throughout the company. All of the employees in Singapore have Singapore Personal Access (SingPass) identification accounts. You are expected to integrate their SingPass IDs with their user identification. You cannot find an existing user property field that is appropriate for holding the SingPass. Furthermore, you are not allowed to deviate from Contoso Pharmaceutical's User Account Name and Location Policy, which specifies the following:

- Each user account should consist of a unique sequential four-digit number, followed by a hyphen, a location designator, another hyphen, and two initials from the employee's name. For example, the first user account in the United States is 0001-US-DD, which was created for David Daniels. The second user account in the United States is 0002-US-CS, which was created for Candy Spoon. The first user account in Canada is 0001-Can-AR, which was created for Andy Ruth.

- Each user account should be placed in an OU that represents the user's physical location. For example, the user accounts for network users located in Mexico should be placed in the Mexico OU.

- Administrator accounts for each location should be unique sequential three-digit numbers, followed by a hyphen and a location designator. For example, the first three administrator accounts in Canada are named 001-Can, 002-Can, and 003-Can.

- All administrator accounts should be maintained in the default Users container.

The location designators are as shown in Table B-1.

Table B-1
Location Designators for Contoso Pharmaceuticals

Location	Designator
United States	US
Canada	Can
Mexico	Mex
Singapore	Sing

Based on what you know about Contoso Pharmaceuticals, answer each of the following questions:

1. Tai Yee is the first network user account that must be created in the Singapore OU. What username do you expect to create for Tai Yee? Where would you place Tai Tee's user account in the Active Directory structure?

2. Mike Danseglio, a network administrator from Seattle, Washington, is the first network administrator in Singapore. He is living and working in Singapore for the first year of the operation. He needs an administrator account for the Singapore location. You want to delegate full control of the Singapore OU to Mike. However, you want Mike to have no control over his own account. What do you name his administrator account and where do you create it?

3. What Active Directory administrative units do you expect to create for the Singapore location, based on what already exists for the other locations?

4. Which Active Directory wizard would you use to help distribute the administrative load for the Singapore location? Where do you run this wizard?

5. How do you propose to maintain the SingPass identification for the Singapore employees in the Active Directory database?

6. How will you secure the Active Directory schema against unauthorized extensions or modifications?

7. A security consulting company performs an audit at the U.S. location while you are in Singapore. Your manager calls to say that the board has decided that all local administrator accounts should be renamed so that the account starts with 500, followed by a hyphen and the name of the location. How can you implement this change easily throughout the company?

8. All of the computers in the Singapore location have built-in smart card readers with drivers that are compatible with Windows Server 2008 and Windows XP. If you want to distribute smart card certificates using autoenrollment to all users, what else must be configured?

9. You discover that another administrator has decided to distribute virus-scanning software to the entire company by linking a GPO to the domain. The virus-scanning software is not compatible with the computers in the Singapore location. You have different virus-scanning software that you want to deploy. What can you do to allow this software to be deployed to all other computers in the domain, except the Singapore location?

10. The Singapore location has 10 computers that are dedicated for public use. However, employees with valid network logons might use these computers. Although these systems are physically secure, you want to ensure that an employee using one of these public systems receives the same user settings as any public user. Public users have a special guest account assigned by the receptionist at the Singapore location. What should you do to ensure that the limitations that apply to the special guest user account also apply to any user logging on to the public computers?

11. You want to ensure that users of the public computers are not allowed to fill up the hard disks with materials downloaded from the Internet. However, you want to allow guest users to save some information to these computers. What Group Policy can you use to control public users?

TROUBLESHOOTING A BREAK SCENARIO

In this portion of Troubleshooting Lab B, you must resolve a "break" scenario that was introduced by your instructor or lab assistant. The computers you are assigned to fix are in pairs.

NOTE	*Do not proceed with break instructions until you receive guidance from your instructor. Your instructor or lab assistant will inform you which break scenario you will be performing (Break Scenario 1 or Break Scenario 2) and which computer to use. Your instructor or lab assistant might also have special instructions. Consult with your instructor or lab assistant before proceeding.*

Break Scenario 1

You are a computer consultant who specializes in Active Directory. You are consulting for Contoso Pharmaceuticals. The company has locations in many different countries.

The company network contains 5 member servers running Windows Server 2008, Standard Edition; 200 client computers running Windows XP Professional; and 3 domain controllers running Windows Server 2008, Enterprise Edition. All computers are configured in a single Active Directory site.

You must resolve a configuration problem that affects every computer in the company. Users on the network cannot save more than 10MB of data in their My Documents folders. The company finds this to be an extreme limitation and wants everyone to be able to save as much data as necessary to the My Documents folder, or anywhere else on the computer, without limitations.

NOTE	*Do not modify the Default Domain Controllers Policy or the Default Domain Policy when troubleshooting this problem.*

As you resolve the configuration issues, record the following information:

- A description of the issue

- A list of all the steps taken to diagnose the problem, even those that did not work

- A description of the problem

- A description of the solution

- A list of the resources used to help solve this problem

Break Scenario 2

You are a computer consultant specializing in Active Directory. You are consulting for Contoso Pharmaceuticals. The company has locations in many different countries.

The company network contains 5 member servers running Windows Server 2008, Standard Edition; 200 client computers running Windows XP Professional; and 3 domain controllers running Windows Server 2008, Enterprise Edition. All computers are configured in a single Active Directory site.

You are assigned to resolve a configuration issue that affects a user named Julie, as well as 500 other employees in the company. Julie's My Documents folder is redirected to a central location. However, company policy states that all users' My Documents folders should be maintained on their local computers.

Your solution should not only resolve Julie's problem, it should resolve the problem for all computers and users in the domain.

As you resolve the configuration issues, record the following information:

- A description of the issue

- A list of all the steps taken to diagnose the problem, even those that did not work

- A description of the problem

- A description of the solution

- A list of the resources used to help solve this problem

LAB 9
SOFTWARE DISTRIBUTION

This lab contains the following projects and activities:

Project 9.1   Deploying Software to Users

Project 9.2   Using Software Restriction Policies

Lab Review Questions

Lab Challenge 9.1   Restricting Access to Cmd

Post-Lab Cleanup

BEFORE YOU BEGIN

Lab 9 assumes the following:

- The even-numbered computer must be configured to use the odd-numbered computer as its Preferred DNS Server, as described in Project 1.4.
- Active Directory is installed on the odd-numbered computer, as described in Project 2.2.
- The even-numbered computer must be a member server within the odd-numbered computer's domain, as described in Project 7.1.

> **NOTE** *In this lab, you will see the characters xx, yy, and zz. These directions assume that students are working in pairs, and that each student has a number. One number is odd and the other number is even. For example, the first student pair will consist of RWDC01 as the first odd-numbered computer and RWDC02 as the first even-numbered computer, RWDC03 and RWDC04 as the second student pair, and RWDC05 and RWDC06 as the third student pair. When you see "xx" in this manual, substitute the unique number assigned to the odd-numbered computer in a pair. When you see "yy", substitute the unique number assigned to the even-numbered computer in a pair. **When you see "zz", substitute the number assigned to the computer that you are currently working at, regardless of whether it is odd or even.***

SCENARIO

You are a network administrator for Blue Yonder Airlines. Blue Yonder Airlines has a single Active Directory domain named blueyonderairlines.com. The network has three domain controllers. The domain controllers run Windows Server 2008, Enterprise Edition. The domain has 10 member servers. Two of the member servers run Windows Server 2008, Enterprise Edition, and the rest run Windows Server 2008, Standard Edition. The 400 client computers on the domain run Windows XP Professional.

Corporate management decided that all of the applications throughout the company must be standardized. Furthermore, management published a list of prohibited applications. Your task is to ensure that the standardized applications are deployed appropriately and that prohibited applications are not used.

After completing this lab, you will be able to:

■ Deploy software to users through Group Policy Objects.

■ Deploy Software Restriction Policies to control the use of unauthorized software on your network.

■ Deploy software to computer objects.

Estimated lesson time: 100 minutes

Project 9.1	Deploying Software to Users
Overview	Corporate management decided that users in the domain should be able to install a custom application that has an associated .msi package. In this lab, you will use the netfx.msi tool to represent the software package that your managers want you to distribute.
Outcomes	After completing this project, you will know how to: • Prepare a software distribution share. • Publish software using Group Policy Objects. • Assign software using Group Policy Objects.
Completion time	35 minutes
Precautions	N/A

■ PART A: Preparing the Distribution Share

1. Press Ctrl+Alt+Delete on the odd-numbered computer assigned to you and log on as the default administrator of the domain*xx*.local domain. Your username is Administrator. The password is MSPress#1 or the password that your instructor or lab proctor has assigned to you.

2. On the odd-numbered computer, insert the Windows Server 2008 installation CD-ROM into the CD-ROM drive. Close any Welcome screen that appears.

3. Create a folder named C:\MSI. Right-click the folder and click Share. The File Sharing Window appears. In the Choose People On Your Network dialog box, key **Everyone** and click Add.

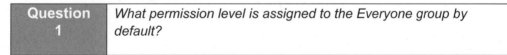

Question 1	*What permission level is assigned to the Everyone group by default?*

4. Click Share, and then click Done.

5. Copy the contents of the the \upgrade\netfx folder on the Windows Server 2008 CD-ROM into the MSI folder.

■ Part B: Publishing Software

1. On the odd-numbered computer, open the Group Policy Management Console.

2. Drill down to Forest: domain*xx*.local→Domains. Right-click domain*xx*.local, and then click Create A GPO In This Domain, And Link It Here. The New GPO screen is displayed.

3. In the Name field, key **SOFTDIST1**. Click OK.

4. Click the plus sign next to Group Policy Objects. Right-click SOFTDIST1 and click Edit.

5. Drill down to User Configuration→Policies→Software Settings. Right-click Software settings and click Properties. The Software Installation Properties dialog box is displayed.

6. Click the Categories tab. Click Add. The Enter New Category screen is displayed. Key **Development Tools**. Click OK twice.

7. Right-click Software Installation, click New, and then click Package. The Open dialog box is displayed.

8. In the File Name dialog box, key **\\rwdcxx\msi** and press Enter. Click Netfx and click Open. The Deploy Software dialog box appears, as shown in Figure 9-1.

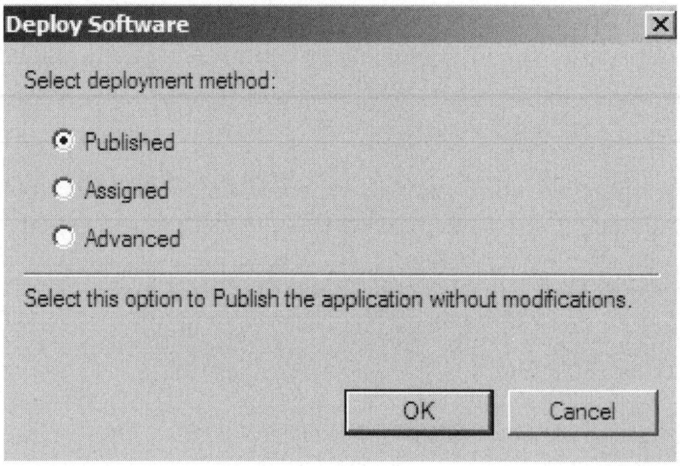

Figure 9-1
Deploy Software dialog box

9. Click Advanced and click OK. After a few moments, the Microsoft .NET Framework 1.1 Properties dialog box appears.

10. Click the Deployment tab. Verify that the Published radio button is selected.

11. Click the Categories tab. Click Select to move the Development Tools category into the Selected Categories column. Click OK.

12. Close the Group Policy Management Editor.

13. Close the Group Policy Management MMC console.

■ Part C: Checking for Published Software

1. On the even-numbered computer, log on as the default administrator of the domain*xx* domain.

2. Click the Start button, click Control Panel, and then click Programs And Features. The Uninstall Or Change A Program window is displayed.

Question 2	*Is the Microsoft .Net Framework 1.1 installed?*

3. Click Install A Program From The Network.

Question 3	*Do you see the Microsoft .Net Framework 1.1 listed?*

4. Close the Programs And Features window.

5. Click the Start button, click All Programs, and then click Administrative Tools.

Question 4	*Do you see the Microsoft .Net Framework 1.1 Configuration icon listed?*

6. Log off of the even-numbered computer.

■ Part D: Assigning Software

1. On the odd-numbered computer, open the Group Policy Management Console. Drill down to Forest: domain*xx*.local→Domains→Group Policy Objects.

2. Right-click the SOFTDIST1 GPO and click Edit. Drill down to User Configuration→Policies→Software Settings→Software Installation.

3. Right-click Microsoft .NET Framework 1.1 and click Properties.

4. Click the Deployment tab. Under the Deployment Type section, click Assigned. In the Deployment Options section, place a checkmark next to Install This Application At Logon. Click OK.

5. Close the Group Policy Management Editor.

6. Close the Group Policy Management MMC snap-in.

■ Part E: Checking for Assigned Software

1. On the even-numbered computer, log on as the default administrator of the domain*xx* domain.

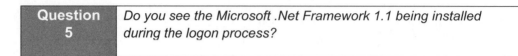

Question 5	Do you see the Microsoft .Net Framework 1.1 being installed during the logon process?

2. Click the Start button, click Control Panel, and then click Programs And Features. The Uninstall Or Change A Program window is displayed.

Question 6	Is the Microsoft .Net Framework 1.1 installed?

3. Close the Programs And Features window.

4. Click the Start button, click All Programs, and then click Administrative Tools.

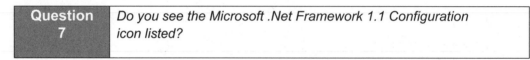

Question 7	Do you see the Microsoft .Net Framework 1.1 Configuration icon listed?

5. Log off of the even-numbered computer.

Project 9.2	Using Software Restriction Policies
Overview	Corporate management decided that too many users spend time browsing the Internet when they should be working. You need to prevent users from accessing Microsoft Internet Explorer. You decide to accomplish this by using Software Restriction Policies.
Outcomes	After completing this project, you will know how to: • Configure a Software Restriction Policy.
Completion time	25 minutes
Precautions	N/A

■ PART A: Create a Software Restriction Policy Path Rule

1. On the odd-numbered computer, log on as the default administrator of the domain*xx*.local domain.

2. Open the Group Policy Management Console.

3. Drill down to Forest: domain*xx*.local→Domains. Right-click domain*xx*.local, and click Create A GPO In This Domain, And Link It Here. The New GPO screen is displayed.

4. In the Name field, key **SRP1**. Click OK.

5. Click the plus sign next to Group Policy Objects. Right-click SRP1 and click Edit.

6. Drill down to User Configuration→Policies→Windows Settings→Security Settings→Software Restriction Policies.

7. Right-click Software Restriction Policies and click New Software Restriction Policies.

8. In the left pane, click Additional Rules. The default rules are displayed in the right pane. Right-click the Additional Rules object and click New Path Rule. The New Path Rule window is displayed.

9. In the Path dialog box, click Browse. The Browse For File Or Folder window is displayed. Browse to the following path and click OK:

    - Computer→C:\→Program Files→Internet Explorer→IEXPLORE.EXE

10. Ensure that the Security Level is set to Disallowed. Click OK.

11. Close the Group Policy Management Editor.

12. Close the Group Policy Management MMC snap-in.

■ PART B: Test the Software Restriction Policy Path Rule

1. On the even-numbered computer, log on as the default administrator of the domain*xx*.local domain.

2. Click the Start button and then click Internet Explorer. A message box is displayed.

3. Read the message and click OK.

Question 8	*Why did the computer fail to open iexplore.exe?*
Question 9	*Can you find a way around this rule that would enable users to run iexplore.exe?*

4. Using the command prompt or Windows Explorer, copy the iexplore.exe executable from C:\Program Files\Internet Explorer to your desktop.

5. Double-click the Internet Explorer icon on your desktop.

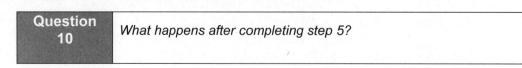

Question 10	What happens after completing step 5?

6. Log off of the even-numbered computer.

■ PART C: Create a Software Restriction Policy Hash Rule

1. On the odd-numbered computer, log on as the default administrator of the domain*xx*.local domain.

2. Open the Group Policy Management Console.

3. Drill down to Forest: domain*xx*.local→Domains. Right-click domain*xx*.local and click Create A GPO In This Domain, And Link It Here. The New GPO screen is displayed.

4. In the Name field, key **SRP2**. Click OK.

5. Click the plus sign next to Group Policy Objects. Right-click SRP2 and click Edit.

6. Drill down to User Configuration→Policies→Windows Settings→Security Settings→Software Restriction Policies.

7. Right-click Software Restriction Policies and click New Software Restriction Policies.

8. In the left window pane, click Additional Rules. The default rules are displayed in the right pane.

9. Right-click the Additional Rules object and click New Hash Rule. The New Hash Rule dialog box is displayed.

10. Click Browse. The Open dialog box is displayed.

11. Browse to the following file and click OK:

    • Computer→C:\ →Program Files→Internet Explorer→IEXPLORE.EXE

12. Ensure that the Security Level is set to Disallowed. Click OK.

13. Close the Group Policy Management Editor.

14. Close the Group Policy Management MMC snap-in.

■ Part D: Testing a Software Restriction Rule Hash Rule

1. On the even-numbered computer, log off and log on as the default administrator of the domain*xx* domain to update Group Policy settings.

2. Double-click the Internet Explorer executable on your Desktop.

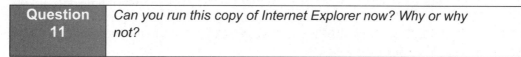

Question 11	*Can you run this copy of Internet Explorer now? Why or why not?*

LAB REVIEW QUESTIONS

Completion time	15 minutes

1. In your own words, describe what you learned by completing this lab.

2. Is the option to publish a software package to a computer available when you create a software package?

3. How can you enable the option Install This Application At Logon in a software package's Deployment tab?

4. What are the advantages and disadvantages of using path rules?

LAB CHALLENGE 9.1	RESTRICTING ACCESS TO CMD
Overview	Although you lock down the desktop using Group Policy, you see copies of cmd.exe on users' desktops. You are not sure how these files are getting there. You want to ensure that users cannot access the Windows command prompt, so you want to create a hash rule to stop users from running this program on the domain.
Outcomes	After completing this project, you will know how to: • Create a Software Restriction Policy hash rule.
Completion time	15 minutes
Precautions	If you do not perform the Lab Challenge, be sure to complete the post-lab cleanup that follows.

Create a GPO named SRP3 and link it to the domain. Edit the GPO and create a hash rule for all computers that disallows the use of cmd.exe

POST-LAB CLEANUP

Overview	Remove all software distribution packages and Software Restriction Policies that you configured in this lab.
Completion time	5 minutes

1. Restart the odd-numbered computer.

2. On the odd-numbered computer, log on as the default administrator of the domain*xx* domain.

3. Open the Group Policy Management Console. Drill down to Forest: domain*xx*.local→Domains→domain*xx*.local.

4. Delete the link to any of the following Group Policy Objects:

    - SOFTDIST1

    - SRP1

    - SRP2

    - SRP3

5. Reboot the even-numbered computer. Log onto the even-numbered computer as the default administrator in the domain*xx* domain. Confirm that you can launch the following executables:

    - c:\windows\system32\mspaint.exe

    - c:\mspaint.exe

    - c:\windows\system32\cmd.exe

6. On the odd-numbered computer, drill down to Forest: domain*xx*.local→Domains→domain*xx*.local→Group Policy Objects.

7. Delete any of the following Group Policy Objects that are present:

   - SOFTDIST1

   - SRP1

   - SRP2

   - SRP3

8. Delete the c:\MSI folder that you created in Project 9.1.

9. Reboot both the odd- and even-numbered computers.

LAB 10
CONTROLLING GROUP POLICY

This lab contains the following projects and activities:

Project 10.1   Deploying Software to Users

Project 10.2   Using Security Filtering

Project 10.3   Working with WMI Filters

Lab Review Questions

Lab Challenge 10.1   Applying WMI Filtering

Post-Lab Cleanup

BEFORE YOU BEGIN

Lab 10 assumes the following:

- The even-numbered computer must be configured to use the odd-numbered computer as its Preferred DNS Server, as described in Project 1.4.
- Active Directory is installed on the odd-numbered computer, as described in Project 2.2.
- The even-numbered computer must be a member server within the odd-numbered computer's domain, as described in Project 7.1.
- Users have the right to log on to domain controllers, as described in Project 5.1.
- The domain functional level must be Windows Server 2008, as described in Project 4.1.

> **NOTE**
>
> *In this lab, you will see the characters xx, yy, and zz. These directions assume that students are working in pairs, and that each student has a number. One number is odd and the other number is even. For example, the first student pair will consist of RWDC01 as the first odd-numbered computer and RWDC02 as the first even-numbered computer, RWDC03 and RWDC04 as the second student pair, and RWDC05 and RWDC06 as the third student pair. When you see "xx" in this manual, substitute the unique number assigned to the odd-numbered computer in a pair. When you see "yy", substitute the unique number assigned to the even-numbered computer in a pair. **When you see "zz", substitute the number assigned to the computer that you are currently working at, regardless of whether it is odd or even.***

SCENARIO

You are a network administrator for Consolidated Messenger. The company network has a single Active Directory domain named consolidatedmessenger.com. It has 5 domain controllers, 10 member servers, and 500 computers. All of the client computers run Microsoft Windows XP Professional. All of the member servers and domain controllers run Windows Server 2008, Standard Edition.

You are responsible for managing Group Policy for Consolidated Messenger. You use Group Policy to deploy and maintain applications, control user access to software, and standardize desktops throughout the company. However, you often find times when you want a policy to apply or not apply to a certain user, computer, or group of users and computers. Management does not want you to change the current Organizational Unit (OU) structure, and you do not want to enable Block Policy Inheritance more than is necessary. Therefore, you are interested in using security filtering and WMI filters as a means of controlling Group Policy deployments.

After completing this lab, you will be able to:

- Use the Group Policy Management Console (GPMC) to configure, link, edit, and delete Group Policy Objects (GPOs).

- Use GPRESULT and RSoP to determine how GPOs are deployed and filtered.

- Implement Group Policy security filtering.

- Configure WMI filters and link them to Group Policy Objects.

Estimated lesson time: 120 minutes

Project 10.1	Deploying Software to Users
Overview	In addition to managing Group Policy, you must often trace the application of GPOs to specific computers or users. Use the GPRESULT and RSOP.MSC tools to troubleshoot GPO deployment issues.
Outcomes	After completing this project, you will know how to: • Create an OU structure. • Use GPRESULT to troubleshoot deployment. • Use RSoP to troubleshoot deployment.
Completion time	35 minutes
Precautions	

In this lab, you will use the Organizational Units (OUs), user accounts, and Group Policy Objects listed in Table 10-1. Your first task is to create this structure.

Table 10-1
Organizational Unit Structure

OU	Users	GPO	GPO Settings	GPO Links
10A	10AUser1 10AUser2	GPOA	Remove Run Enabled	10A
10B	10BUser1 10BUser2	GPOB	Remove Help menu Enabled	10B
10C	10CUser1 10CUser2	GPOC	Remove Search Enabled	10C

■ PART A: Creating the OU Structure

1. Press Ctrl+Alt+Delete on the odd-numbered computer assigned to you and log on as the default administrator of the domainxx.local domain. Your username is Administrator. The password is MSPress#1 or the password that your instructor or lab proctor has assigned to you.

2. Using Active Directory Users And Computers, create three OUs, as listed in Table 10-1. (Reference Project 6.3 for information about creating OUs.) Create OU 10A and OU 10B as top-level OUs in the domainxx.local domain. Create OU 10C as a child OU to OU 10B, as shown in Figure 10-1.

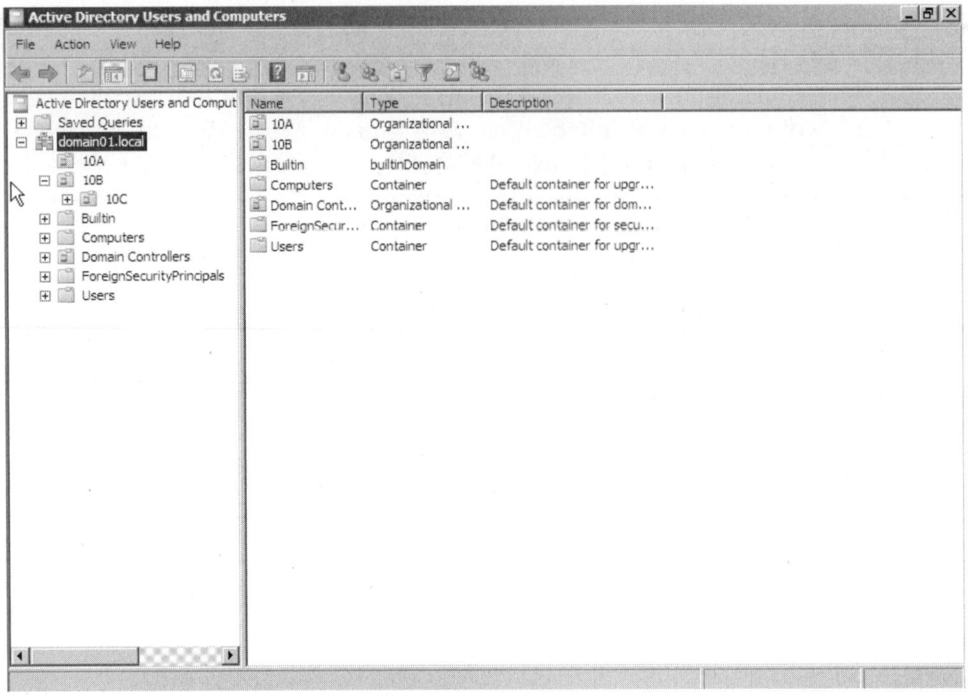

Figure 10-1
Organizational Units

3. Create six user accounts in the appropriate OUs as listed in Table 10-1 (reference Project 4.1.) Set all user passwords to MSPress#1. Do not require users to change their passwords at the next logon.

4. Open the Group Policy Management Console. Drill down to Forest: domain*xx*.local→Domains→domain*xx*.local→10A. Right-click 10A and click Create A GPO In This Domain, And Link It Here. The New GPO dialog box is displayed.

5. In the Name field, key **GPOA**. Click OK.

6. Expand the Group Policy Objects node. Right-click GPOA and click Edit. The Group Policy Management Editor is displayed.

7. In the left pane, drill down to User Configuration→Policies→Administrative Templates→Start Menu And Taskbar.

8. In the right pane, double-click Remove Run Menu From Start Menu. The Remove Run Menu From Start Menu Properties dialog box is displayed.

9. Select the Enabled radio button and click OK.

10. Close the Group Policy Management Editor, but do not close the Group Policy Management MMC.

11. Use the Group Policy Management MMC to create and link GPOB to the 10B OU. Edit GPOB and enable the Remove Help Menu From Start Menu setting.

12. Use the Group Policy Management MMC to create and link GPOC to the 10C OU. Edit GPOC and enable the Remove Search Link From Start Menu setting.

■ PART B: Using GPRESULT to Troubleshoot Deployment

1. On the odd-numbered computer, open a command-prompt window. Key **gpupdate /force** and press Enter. Log off of the odd-numbered computer and then log on as 10AUser1 of the domain*xx* domain.

2. Click the Start button, click All Programs, click Accessories, and then click Command Prompt. Key **gpresult /r** and then press Enter. After a few minutes, output will be displayed in the command-prompt window.

3. Look at the Applied Group Policy Objects section and verify that GPOA is listed.

4. Close the command-prompt window.

5. On the even-numbered computer, open a command-prompt window. Key **gpupdate /force** and then press Enter. Log on as 10AUser2 of the domain*xx* domain. Repeat steps 2 through 4.

■ Part C: Use RSoP to Troubleshoot Deployment

1. On the odd-numbered computer, log off and log on as 10CUser1 of the domain*xx* domain.

2. Click the Start button, key **rsop.msc,** and then click OK. When prompted, reenter the password for the 10CUser1 user account. A Group Policy error message is displayed, indicating that the user does not have the administrative permissions to see the security settings applied to the computer. However, this user is allowed to see the settings applying to the user account.

3. Read the error message and click Close. The Resultant Set Of Policy console is displayed.

4. In the left window pane, expand Administrative Templates and click Start Menu And Taskbar.

5. Read the contents in the right pane. You should see only the GPO settings that apply to this user account.

Question 1	What are the names of the settings that apply to this user account?

6. In the right pane, double-click Remove Help Menu From Start Menu. The Remove Search link From Start Menu Properties dialog box is displayed.

7. Click the Precedence tab, as shown in Figure 10-2.

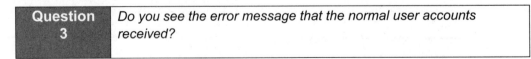

Figure 10-2
Remove Help Menu from Start Menu dialog box

| Question 2 | What GPO name do you see listed here? |

8. Click OK to close the Remove Help Menu From Start Menu Properties dialog box.

9. Close the Resultant Set Of Policy console.

10. On the even-numbered computer, log off and log on as 10CUser2 of the domain*xx* domain. Repeat steps 2 through 9.

11. On the odd-numbered computer, log off and log on as the default administrator of the domain*xx* domain.

12. Run RSoP.MSC.

| Question 3 | Do you see the error message that the normal user accounts received? |

13. Close the Resultant Set Of Policy console.

Project 10.2	Using Security Filtering
Overview	You have a GPO that you want to apply to only members of the 10BGroup1 in the 10B OU. You want to try security filtering to prevent this GPO from applying to other users.
Outcomes	After completing this project, you will know how to: • Configure security group filtering.
Completion time	20 minutes
Precautions	N/A

■ **PART A: Configuring Security Group Filtering**

1. On the odd-numbered computer, log on as the default administrator of the domain*xx*.local domain. Open Active Directory Users And Computers.

2. Expand domain*xx*.local in the left pane.

3. Right-click the 10B OU, click New, and then click Group. The New Object – Group dialog box is displayed.

4. In the Group Name text box, key **10BGroup1** and click OK.

5. Right-click the group you just created and select Properties. Click the Members tab. Add 10BUser1 to the 10BGroup1 group object and click OK.

6. Open the Group Policy Management Console. Drill down to
    Forest: domain*xx*.local→Domains→domain*xx*.local→Group Policy Objects.

7. Select the GPOB GPO. In the Security Filtering section, highlight Authenticated Users and click Remove. Click OK to confirm the removal.

8. Click Add. The Select Computer, User, Or Group dialog box is displayed. Key **10BGroup1** and click OK.

9. Close the Group Policy Management MMC snap-in.

10. Log off of both the odd-numbered and even-numbered computers.

■ PART B: Testing Security Filtering

1. On the odd-numbered computer, log on as the default administrator in the domain*xx* domain. Open a command-prompt window. Key **gpupdate /force** and press Enter. Log off of the odd-numbered computer and log back on as 10BUser1.

2. Run GPRESULT /r from a command-prompt window and review the objects listed in the Applied Group Policy Objects section. (Refer to Project 10.1 for additional information about GPRESULT.)

3. Click the Start button.

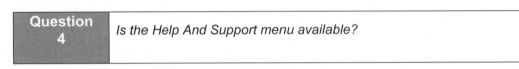

Question 4	Is the Help And Support menu available?

4. On the even-numbered computer, log on as 10BUser2 of the domain*xx* domain.

5. Run GPRESULT /r from a command-prompt window and review the objects listed in the Applied Group Policy Objects section. (Refer to Project 10.1 for additional information about GPRESULT.)

6. Run RSoP.MSC to validate which configuration settings affect 10BUser2. (Refer to Project 10.1 for additional information about RSoP.MSC.)

Question 5	Why does 10BUser2 have a Help And Support menu in the Start menu, but 10BUser1 does not?
Question 6	If you want the GPO to apply to all Authenticated Users in the 10B OU and subordinate OUs except the members of 10BGroup1, what must you do differently?

Project 10.3   Working with WMI Filters

Overview	You want to remove the last logged on user name from the Log On To Windows dialog box for several computers on your network. All of these computers already have the Print Spooler service disabled. You decide to create a GPO with a WMI filter to remove the user name from the Log On To Windows dialog box if the Print Spooler service is disabled.
Outcomes	After completing this project, you will know how to: • Create and configure a WMI filter.
Completion time	25 minutes
Precautions	N/A

■ PART A: Creating a WMI Filter

1. On the even-numbered computer, log on as the default administrator of the domain*xx* domain.

2. Open a command-prompt window, key **net stop spooler,** and then press Enter. This will stop the Print Spooler service.

3. Key in **sc config start spooler= disabled** and press Enter. The [SC] ChangeServiceConfig SUCCESS message is displayed.

4. On the odd-numbered computer, log on as the default administrator of the domain*xx* domain.

5. Open the Group Policy Management Console. Drill down to Forest: domain*xx*.local→Domains→domain*xx*.local. Right-click domain*xx*.local and click Create A GPO In This Domain, And Link It Here.

6. Key **GPOD** into the Name text box and click OK. In the left pane. Expand the Group Policy Objects node.

7. Right-click GPOD in the right pane and click Edit. The Group Policy Management Editor is displayed.

8. In the left pane, navigate to Computer Configuration→Policies→Windows Settings→Security Settings→Local Policies→Security Options.

9. In the right pane, double-click Interactive Logon: Do Not Display Last User Name.

10. Select the Define This Policy Setting checkbox and then select the Enabled radio button.

11. Click OK, and then close the Group Policy Management Editor.

12. In the left pane of the Group Policy Mangement MMC console, right-click WMI Filters and click New. The New WMI Filter dialog box is displayed.

13. Key **Print Spooler Disabled** into the Name text box of the New WMI Filter dialog box.

14. Click Add. The WMI Query dialog box is displayed.

15. Key in **Select * from Win32_Service where Name='schedule' and startmode='disabled'** in the Query text box and click OK.

16. Click Save in the New WMI Filter dialog box.

17. In the left pane, click GPOD.

18. In the right pane, click the drop-down box below the WMI Filtering heading and select the Print Spooler Disabled WMI filter. A Group Policy Management message is displayed, asking you to confirm this change. Click Yes.

19. Close the Group Policy Management MMC console.

■ PART B: Testing the WMI Filter

1. On the even-numbered computer, open a command-prompt window.

2. Key **gpupdate /force** into the command-prompt window and press Enter.

3. Close the command-prompt window and log off.

4. Press Ctrl+Alt+Delete to display the Log On To Windows dialog box.

Question 7	Do you see the user name of the last person to log on to this computer? Explain your results.

5. On the odd-numbered computer, open a command-prompt window, key **gpupdate /force** and press Enter.

6. Key **wmic service where startmode='auto' get name** and press Enter. You will see a report of services configured to run automatically at startup. Notice the list of services that are configured to start automatically includes Spooler, which is the Print Spooler service.

7. Close the command-prompt window and log off.

8.   Press Ctrl+Alt+Delete to display the Log On To Windows dialog box.

Question 8	*Do you see the user name of the last person to log on to this computer? Explain your results.*

LAB REVIEW QUESTIONS

Completion time	15 minutes

1.   In your own words, describe what you learned by completing this lab.

2.   When you want to filter a GPO based on file system attributes, installed services, or running services, what type of filtering do you use?

3.   When you want to filter a GPO based on group membership, what type of filter do you use?

4.   What tools can you use to investigate the application of GPOs for a particular computer or user account?

5.   When running GPRESULT or GPMC using a nonadministrative account, what information is unavailable?

LAB CHALLENGE 10.1	APPLYING WMI FILTERING
Overview	Your task is to disable the Computer Browser (browser) service on the even-numbered computer. Create a GPO named GPOE. In GPOE, configure the security option Interactive Logon: Do Not Require Ctrl+Alt+Del to be enabled. Create a WMI filter so that computers that do not have the Computer Browser service enabled do not receive GPOE. Verify that the even-numbered computer receives this policy and the odd-numbered computer does not.
Outcomes	After completing this project, you will know how to: • Apply a WMI filter.
Completion time	25 minutes
Precautions	If you do not perform the Lab Challenge, be sure to complete the post-lab cleanup that follows.

Create a GPO named SRP3 and link it to the domain. Edit the GPO and create a hash rule for all computers that disallows the use of cmd.exe.

POST-LAB CLEANUP	
Overview	Remove all Group Policy Objects and WMI Filters that you configured in this lab.
Outcomes	After completing this project, you will know how to: • Remove Group Policy Objects and WMI filters.
Completion time	5 minutes
Precautions	N/A

■ PART A: Enable the Computer Browser and Task Scheduler Services on the Even-Numbered Computer

1. On the even-numbered computer, log on as the default administrator of the domain*xx* domain.

2. Open a command-prompt window.

3. Key **sc config browser start= auto** and press Enter.

4. Key **sc config spooler start spooler= auto** and press Enter.

5. Close the command-prompt window.

■ PART B: Remove All GPOs That You Created During This Lab

1. On the odd-numbered computer, log on as the default administrator of the domain*xx* domain.

2. Open the Group Policy Management Console. Drill down to Forest: domain*xx*.local→Domains→domain*xx*.local.

3. Delete the link to any of the following Group Policy Objects:

    •   GPOA

    •   GPOB

    •   GPOC

    •   GPOD

    •   GPOE

4. On both the even- and odd-numbered computers, open a command-prompt window, key **gpupdate /force**, and then press Enter.

5. On the odd-numbered computer, drill down to Forest: domain*xx*.local→Domains→domain*xx*.local→Group Policy Objects.

6. Delete any of the following Group Policy Objects that are present:

    - GPOA

    - GPOB

    - GPOC

    - GPOD

    - GPOE

7. Reboot both the odd- and even-numbered computers.

LAB 11
DISASTER RECOVERY AND MAINTENANCE

This lab contains the following projects and activities:

Project 11.1   Installing a Replica Domain Controller

Project 11.2   Resolving Replication Issues

Project 11.3   Performing a System State Data Backup

Project 11.4   Compacting the Database

Project 11.5   Performing an Authoritative Restore

Lab Review Questions

Lab Challenge 11.1   Restoring a User Account

Post-Lab Cleanup

BEFORE YOU BEGIN

Lab 11 assumes the following:

- The even-numbered computer must be configured to use the odd-numbered computer as its Preferred DNS Server, as described in Project 1.4.
- Active Directory is installed on the odd-numbered computer, as described in Project 2.2.

- The even-numbered computer must be a member server within the odd-numbered computer's domain, as described in Project 7.1.
- Users have the right to log onto domain controllers, as described in Project 5.1.
- To perform a System State backup, each computer must be configured with a second hard drive partition.

> **NOTE**
>
> *In this lab, you will see the characters xx, yy, and zz. These directions assume that students are working in pairs, and that each student has a number. One number is odd and the other number is even. For example, the first student pair will consist of RWDC01 as the first odd-numbered computer and RWDC02 as the first even-numbered computer, RWDC03 and RWDC04 as the second student pair, and RWDC05 and RWDC06 as the third student pair. When you see "xx" in this manual, substitute the unique number assigned to the odd-numbered computer in a pair. When you see "yy", substitute the unique number assigned to the even-numbered computer in a pair. When you see "zz", substitute the number assigned to the computer that you are currently working at, regardless of whether it is odd or even.***

SCENARIO

You are a network administrator for Humongous Insurance. The company uses a single Active Directory domain named humongousinsurance.com. The domain has 16 Active Directory sites worldwide. You are the lead administrator for Main_Site. You are responsible for all Active Directory–related issues. You must ensure that all sites have proper load-balancing and fault tolerance. Furthermore, you must resolve any discrepancies with the Active Directory database.

After completing this lab, you will be able to:

- Create a second domain controller within an Active Directory domain.

- Recognize and resolve Active Directory replication issues.

- Perform System State backups and restores.

Estimated lesson time: 190 minutes

Project 11.1   Installing a Replica Domain Controller

Overview	You want to improve fault tolerance and performance on your domain. You decide to install an additional domain controller in the domain*xx*.local domain.
Outcomes	After completing this project, you will know how to: • Install an additional domain controller in a Windows Server 2008 domain.
Completion time	20 minutes
Precautions	N/A

1. Press Ctrl+Alt+Delete on the even-numbered computer assigned to you and log on as the default administrator of the domain*xx*.local domain. Your username is Administrator. The password is MSPress#1 or the password that your instructor or lab proctor has assigned to you.

2. If the Server Manager console does not appear automatically, click Start and then click Server Manager.

3. In the left pane, select Roles. In the right pane, click Add Roles.

4. Click Next to bypass the initial Welcome screen. The Select Server Roles screen is displayed.

5. Place a checkmark next to Active Directory Domain Services. Click Next. The Active Directory Domain Services screen is displayed.

6. Read the introductory information to Active Directory Domain Services and click Next. The Confirm Installation Selections screen is displayed.

7. Read the confirmation information to prepare for the installation. Click Install to install the AD Domain Services role. The Installation Results screen is displayed.

8. Click Close This Wizard And Launch The Active Directory Domain Services Installation Wizard (Dcpromo.exe). The Welcome To The Active Directory Domain Services Installation Wizard screen is displayed.

9. Click Next twice to continue. The Choose A Deployment Configuration screen is displayed.

10. Click the Existing Forest radio button, click Add A Domain Controller To An Existing Domain, and then click Next. The Network Credentials screen is displayed.

11. In the Type The Name Of Any Domain In The Forest Where You Plan To Install This Domain Controller text box, key **domain*xx*.local,** if it does not automatically appear. Click Next to continue. The Select A Domain screen is displayed.

12. Select the domain*xx*.local domain and click Next. The Select A Site screen is displayed.

13. Accept the default value and click Next. The Additional Domain Controller Options screen is displayed.

14. Remove the checkmark next to DNS Server and click Next. The Location For Database, Log Files, And SYSVOL screen is displayed.

15. Accept the default selections and click Next to continue. The Directory Services Restore Mode Administrator Password screen is displayed.

16. Key **MSPress#1** in the Password and Confirm Password text boxes. Click Next to continue. The Summary screen is displayed.

17. Review your installation choices and click Next to continue. The Active Directory Domain Services Installation Wizard screen is displayed, indicating that the Active Directory Domain Service is being installed. Upon completion of installation, the Completing The Active Directory Domain Services Installation Wizard screen is displayed.

18. Click Finish. When prompted, click Restart Now to restart the newly configured domain controller.

Project 11.2	Resolving Replication Issues
Overview	Your manager sends instructions to two different administrators to perform conflicting tasks. These administrators perform the tasks on two different domain controllers in two different sites. After replication occurs, you notice odd results in the Active Directory Users And Computers node.
Outcomes	After completing this project, you will know how to: • Recognize and respond to Active Directory replication issues.
Completion time	30 minutes
Precautions	N/A

■ PART A: Simulate the Issue

1. On the even-numbered computer, log on as the default administrator of the domain*xx*.local domain. Open Active Directory Users And Computers.

2. Verify that you are connected to the even-numbered computer within the ADUC console. To do so, right-click the Active Directory Users And Computers node in the left pane and then click Change Domain Controller. Verify that Current Domain Controller is set to RWDC*yy*.domain*xx*.local. If it is not, you should select RWDC*yy*.domain*xx*.local in the Change To This Domain Controller or AD LDS instance box. Click OK.

3. Create a new OU named Administration in the domain*xx*.local domain.

4. On the odd-numbered computer, log on as the default administrator of the domain*xx*.local domain. Open the Active Directory Users And Computers node.

5. Ensure that you are connected to the odd-numbered computer within the ADUC console. To do so, right-click the Active Directory Users And Computers node in the left pane and then click Change Domain Controller. Verify that Current Domain Controller is set to RWDC*xx*.domain*xx*.local. If it is not, you should select RWDC*xx*.domain*xx*.local in the Change To This Domain Controller box. Click OK.

6. Ensure that the Administration OU has replicated to the odd-numbered computer. If you do not want to wait for replication to occur, then force replication using the steps in Project 3.1.

7. On the even-numbered computer, simulate a replication delay by disabling the network connection. To disable the network connection, click Start, and then click Control Panel. Double-click Network And Sharing Center. In the left pane, click Manage Network Connections. Right-click the Local Area Connection icon and click Disable. This prevents the two domain controllers from replicating.

8. On the odd-numbered computer, create three new user accounts inside the Administration OU. Name the user accounts Misty, Samantha, and Denise. For all of these accounts, use MSPress#1 as the password and clear the User Must Change Password At Next Logon checkbox.

9. On the odd-numbered computer, create a new OU named Accounting in the domain*xx*.local domain.

10. Disable the network connection on the odd-numbered computer.

11. Enable the even-numbered computer's network connection. To enable the network connection, click Start, and then click Control Panel. Double-click Network And Sharing Center. In the left pane, click Manage Network Connections. Right-click the Local Area Connection icon and click Enable.

12. On the even-numbered computer, create a new OU named Accounting in the domain*xx*.local domain.

13. Create two new user accounts inside the Accounting OU. Name the user accounts Wedge and Wood. For both of these accounts, use MSPress#1 as the password and clear the User Must Change Password At Next Logon checkbox.

 You will experience slow performance when creating the users on the even-numbered computer while the odd-numbered computer's network connection is disabled, because the odd-numbered computer is the only domain controller that is running the DNS Server service.

14. On the even-numbered computer, delete the Administration OU from the domain.

15. Enable the network connection on the odd-numbered computer to allow the two domain controllers to replicate their changes. If you do not want to wait, force replication.

■ PART B: Discovering and Resolving the Issue

You discover that the Administration OU that you created earlier with several user accounts is now missing. You learn that an administrator at another site deleted the Administration OU when there were no user accounts in the OU. You also learn that the other administrator created an OU named Accounting at nearly the same time that you did. You know there is a replication delay between the two domain controllers, so you think there may be two Accounting OUs.

To view the replication issue:

1. On the odd-numbered computer, close the Active Directory User And Computers node and then open it again. When the console reappears, you should see that the

Administration OU is gone. The console displays two Accounting OUs, one of which has additional characters, as shown in Figure 11-1.

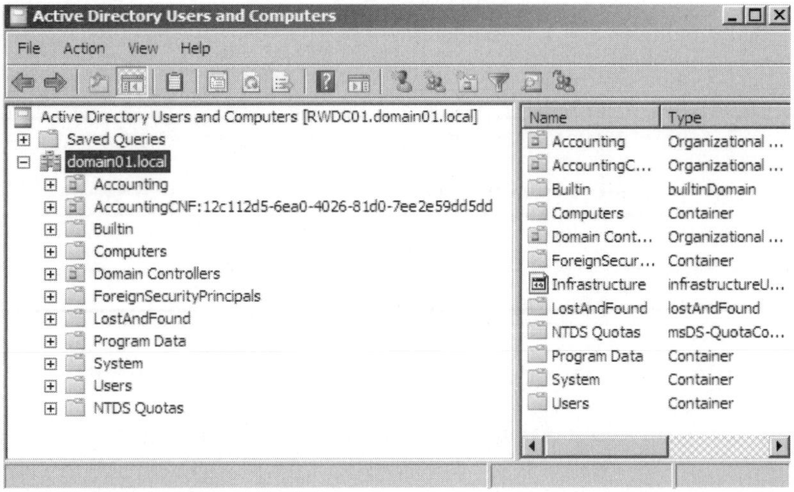

Figure 11-1
Two Accounting OUs displayed

2. In the Active Directory Users And Computers console, ensure that the Advanced Features view option is enabled. To verify that this option is enabled, click the View menu and confirm that a checkmark is displayed next to Advanced Features.

Question 1	What does the alphanumeric string appended to the Accounting OU name represent?

3. In the left pane, click the LostAndFound container. In this container, you should see the three user accounts (Denise, Misty, and Samantha) you created earlier.

Question 2	Why are these three user accounts in the LostAndFound container?

4. To resolve the loss of the Administration OU, create a new Administration OU. Then, move the users from the LostAndFound container to the new Administration OU.

5. To resolve the Accounting OU problem, you should first determine if either OU contains any objects. If the Accounting OU with the alphanumeric string appended to the name has unique objects, such as users Wedge and Wood, move all of the objects to the Accounting OU. Then, delete the Accounting OU conflict object with the CNF string appended.

6. Close Active Directory Users And Computers on both domain controllers.

Project 11.3	Performing a System State Data Backup
Overview	You are about to make some configuration changes to your Active Directory database. You want to have a current System State data backup before you proceed.
Outcomes	After completing this project, you will know how to: • Create a System State backup of a Windows Server 2008 computer.
Completion time	30 minutes
Precautions	N/A

■ PART A: Installing the Windows Server Backup Feature

1. Log onto the RWDC*zz* computer as the default administrator of the domain*xx* domain.

2. If the Server Manager window does not appear automatically, click Start, and then click Server Manager.

3. In the left pane, browse to Features. In the right pane, click Add Features. The Select Features window is displayed.

4. Place a checkmark next to the following features:

    • Windows Powershell

    • Windows Server Backup Features→Windows Server Backup

    • Windows Server Backup Features→Command-line tools

5. Click Next, and then click Install to add the Windows Server Backup feature.

6. Click Close when the installation has completed.

■ PART B: Perform the System State Backup

1. Click Start, click Administrative Tools, and then click Windows Server Backup.

2. Click Action, and then click Backup Once. The Backup Options Wizard is displayed.

3. Click Next to begin performing a one-time backup. If this is the first backup you have performed, you might see the warning shown in Figure 11-2.

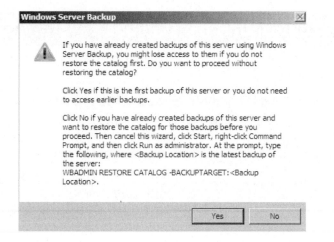

Figure 11-2
Warning dialog box

4. Click Yes to acknowledge the warning and continue. The Select Backup Configuration screen is displayed.

5. Click Custom and then click Next. The Select Backup Items window is displayed.

6. Verify that the second hard drive on the RWDC*zz* computer has been deselected and then click Next. The Specify Destination Type window is displayed.

7. Click Local Drives and then click Next. The *Select Backup Destination* window is displayed.

8. In the Backup Destination dropdown list, confirm that the second hard drive on the RWDC*xx* computer is selected, and then click Next. The Specify Advanced Option window is displayed.

9. Read the description of the VSS copy backup and click Next. The Confirmation screen is displayed.

10. Click Backup to begin the backup process.

11. Click Close when the backup completes. Close the Windows Server Backup console.

Project 11.4	Compacting the Database
Overview	You want to reduce the space that Active Directory occupies on your domain controller.
Outcomes	After completing this project, you will know how to: • Perform an offline defragmentation of the Active Directory database.
Completion time	30 minutes
Precautions	You can perform this exercise on one or both computers.

1. Log onto the computer as the default administrator of the domain*xx*.local domain.

2. Open a command-prompt window. To enable Directory Services Restore Mode on the next reboot, key **bcdedit /set safeboot dsrepair**, and then press Enter.

3. Close the command-prompt window and restart the computer.

4. When the computer restarts, log onto the local computer (not the domain) using the Directory Services Restore Mode username and password. The username should be Administrator and the password should be MSPress#1. The Windows Desktop should indicate that the domain controller is operating in Safe Mode.

5. Open a command-prompt window, key **NTDSUTIL**, and press Enter.

6. Key **activate instance ntds** and press Enter.

7. Key **files** and press Enter. The File Maintenance prompt is displayed.

8. Key **?** and press Enter. Notice that you have several options at this prompt. You can check the Active Directory database integrity, move the database, and move the database log files.

9. Key **info** and press Enter. This command displays the current location of the Acitve Directory database (ntds.dit), the backup directory, and the log files directory.

10. To perform offline compaction of the database, key **compact to c:** and press Enter. The database is compacted and you are given directions to replace the existing database.

11. Key **quit** and press Enter. The ntdsutil prompt is displayed.

12. Key **quit** again and press Enter. You are returned to the command prompt.

13. Key **move %systemroot%\ntds\ntds.dit c:\ntds.old** and press Enter. This saves your old Active Directory database in case you have trouble with the newly compacted database. You can delete this copy after you verify that the newly compacted database loads correctly after you restart the computer. Otherwise, you can use the ntds.old file to replace the compacted database.

14. Key **move %systemroot%\ntds*.log c:** and press Enter. This command moves the former Active Directory database log files to the c:\ drive.

15. Key **move c:\ntds.dit %systemroot%\ntds\ntds.dit** and press Enter. This command places the newly compacted database in the appropriate location to load when you restart the computer.

16. Key **dir c:\ntds.old** and press Enter. Statistics for the previous copy of the Active Directory database are displayed.

17. Key **dir %systemroot%\ntds\ntds.dit** and press Enter. The Active Directory database is compacted. Statistics for the newly compacted Active Directory database are displayed. Compare the size of the ntds.old file to the size of the ntds.dit file. You might not see a size difference between the compacted file and the original file, because the database in the lab has not had a chance to become fragmented. On a computer that hosts an Active Directory database that experiences a large number of changes, you could reduce the amount of space that the Active Directory database occupied with the compacting process.

18. To remove the Directory Services Restore Mode boot option, key **bcdedit /deletevalue safeboot** and press Enter. Restart the domain controller.

> **NOTE**
>
> *If you encounter Directory Services errors in the Windows Event Viewer when you restart the computer, you will need to restart again in Directory Services Restore mode. You will then open a command-prompt window and key **move c:\ntds.old %systemroot%\ntds.ntds.dit**, which will replace the compacted copy of the database with the old copy of the Active Directory database. You will also need to copy the old log files from the c:\ drive to the %systemroot%\ntds folder.*

19. If the computer starts properly without errors, log on as the default administrator of the domain*xx* domain. Open a command-prompt window. Key **del c:\ntds.old c:\res*.log c:\edb*.log** and press Enter. This will delete the old Active Directory database and log files. Close the command-prompt window.

Project 11.5	Performing an Authoritative Restore
Overview	You accidentally delete an OU and all of its user accounts. You want to restore the OU using an authoritative restore.
Outcomes	After completing this project, you will know how to: • Use wbadmin and ntdsutil to perform an authoritative restore of Active Directory.
Completion time	30 minutes
Precautions	You can perform this project from either computer, but not from both. You must first complete Project 11.3 on the computer that you select to use for this exercise.

1. Verify that you are logged on as the default administrator of the domain*xx*.local domain. Open Active Directory Users And Computers.

2. Delete the Administration OU and all of its contents. Close Active Directory Users And Computers.

3. Restart the computer in Directory Services Restore Mode. Log onto the local computer (not the domain) using the Directory Services Restore Mode administrator username and password. The administrator username should be Administrator and the password should be MSPress#1.

4. Open a command-prompt window. Key **wbadmin get versions** to obtain the date and timestamp of the backup that you performed in Project 11.3.

5. Key **wbadmin start systemstaterecovery –version:mm/dd/yyyy-hh:ss**, substituting the month, day, year, hour and second of the backup that you performed. You will see the screen shown in Figure 11-3.

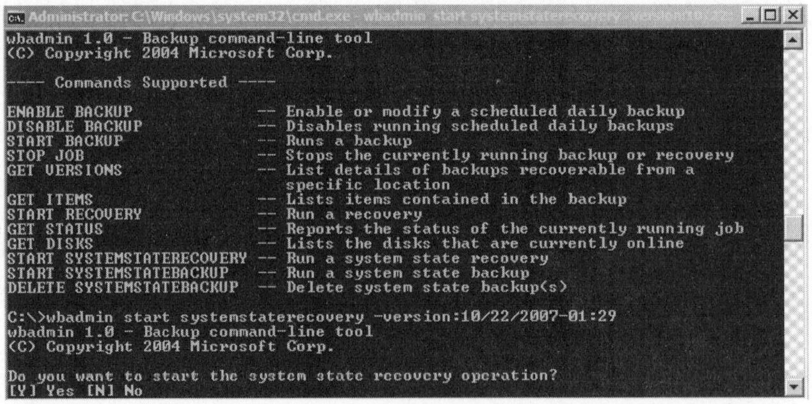

Figure 11-3
Beginning the restore process

6. Key **Y** and press Enter to begin the restore process. You might see a warning message before the restore begins. Key **Y** again and press Enter.

7. Allow several minutes for the restore to complete. After the restore is completed, you will see a message instructing you to restart your system. You must perform the authoritative restore before restarting. Key **ntdsutil** and press Enter.

8. Key **activate instance ntds** and press Enter.

9. Key **authoritative restore** and press Enter.

10. Key **restore subtree ou=Administration,dc=domain*xx*,dc=local** and press Enter. An Authoritative Restore Confirmation dialog box is displayed.

11. Click Yes. The operation may take a few minutes to complete. You will see a message stating that the authoritative restore has been completed successfully.

12. Key **quit** and press Enter. Key **quit** again and press Enter. You are returned to the command prompt.

13. Restart the computer in normal mode. Log onto the computer as the default administrator of the domain*xx*.local domain.

14. Open Active Directory Users And Computers. The Administration OU should be visible in the console. Click the Administration OU to display its contents.

> **NOTE** *If you did not perform an authoritative restore, the Administraion OU might reappear for a short period, but the replication process would eventually remove it from the domain because the other domain controller would have the deletion marked as a more recent change.*

> **Question 3** *Were the Denise, Misty, and Samantha user accounts restored with the Administration OU?*

15. Close the Active Directory Users And Computers console.

LAB REVIEW QUESTIONS

Completion time	15 minutes

1. In your own words, describe what you learned by completing this lab.

2. If you wanted to restore the entire Active Directory database authoritatively, what command in ntdsutil do you use instead of restore subtree?

3. To perform an authoritative restore, what startup option do you select?

4. When performing an authoritative restore, in what mode do you restore your System State data? What tool do you immediately run after the restore?

5. How do you configure a domain controller to start in Directory Services Restore Mode on the next bootup?

6. What command do you key at the File Maintenance prompt if you want to compact your Active Directory database to a directory named database in the root of the C drive?

LAB CHALLENGE 11.1	RESTORING A USER ACCOUNT
Overview	After you delete the Misty user account, you realize that you need the account. You want to bring back the Misty user account by using an authoritative restore. Use the System State backup performed in Project 11.3 to restore the Misty user account. Verify that the account is restored to the Administration OU.
Outcomes	After completing this exercise, you will know how to: • Perform an authoritative restore.
Completion time	30 minutes
Precautions	If you do not perform the Lab Challenge, you must still perform the Post-Lab Cleanup.

POST-LAB CLEANUP	
Overview	Roll back all changes made in this lab.
Outcomes	After completing this project, you will know how to: • Demote a domain contoller in an Active Directory domain.
Completion time	20 minutes
Precautions	N/A

■ PART A: Demote the Domain*yy*.Local Domain

1.   On the even-numbered computer, log on as the default administrator of the domain*xx* domain.

2.   Click Start, key **dcpromo**, and press Enter. The Active Directory Installation Wizard is displayed.

3.   Click Next. If prompted that the domain controller is a global catalog server, click OK. The *Remove Active Directory* page is displayed.

4.   Verify that the This Server Is The Last Domain Controller in the Domain checkbox is cleared and press Next. The *Administrator Password* page is displayed.

5.   Key **MSPress#1** in the New Administrator and Confirm Password text boxes. Click Next. The *Summary* page is displayed.

6.   Confirm your selections. Click Next. The removal of Active Directory begins. This process will take several minutes. When the process is complete, the *Completing The Active Directory Installation Wizard* page is displayed.

7.   Click Finish. The Active Directory Installation Wizard message appears, asking you to restart the computer.

8.   Click Restart Now to complete the process.

■ PART B: Remove the Active Directory Domain Services Role

1.   Log onto the RWDC*yy* computer as the local administrator. If the Server Manager console does not appear automatically, click the Start button, and then click Server Manager.

2.   Drill down to Roles in the left pane. In the right pane, click Remove Roles.

3.   Follow the prompts in the Remove Roles wizard to remove the Active Directory Domain Services role. Restart the RWDC*yy* computer when prompted.

LAB 12
CONFIGURING NAME RESOLUTION AND ADDITIONAL SERVICES

This lab contains the following projects and activities:

Project 12.1   Installing a New Active Directory Domain

Project 12.2   Creating a Reverse Lookup Zone

Project 12.3   Configuring Secondary Zones and Zone Transfers

Project 12.4   Installing the Rights Management Service Role

Lab Review Questions

Lab Challenge 12.1   Creating a CNAME Record

Post-Lab Cleanup

BEFORE YOU BEGIN

Lab 12 assumes the following:

- The even-numbered computer must be configured to use the odd-numbered computer as its Preferred DNS Server, as described in Project 1.4.
- Active Directory is installed on the odd-numbered computer, as described in Project 2.2.
- The even-numbered computer must be a member server within the odd-numbered computer's domain, as described in Project 7.1.
- Users have the right to log onto domain controllers, as described in Project 5.1.
- To perform a System State backup, at least one computer has been configured with a second hard drive partition.

> **NOTE**
>
> *In this lab, you will see the characters xx, yy, and zz. These directions assume that students are working in pairs, and that each student has a number. One number is odd and the other number is even. For example, the first student pair will consist of RWDC01 as the first odd-numbered computer and RWDC02 as the first even-numbered computer, RWDC03 and RWDC04 as the second student pair, and RWDC05 and RWDC06 as the third student pair. When you see "xx" in this manual, substitute the unique number assigned to the odd-numbered computer in a pair. When you see "yy", substitute the unique number assigned to the even-numbered computer in a pair.* **When you see "zz", substitute the number assigned to the computer that you are currently working at, regardless of whether it is odd or even.**

SCENARIO

You are a network administrator for Trey Research. The company uses a single Active Directory domain named treyresearch.net. The domain has a dozen Active Directory sites located throughout the United States. You are responsible for all Active Directory– and name-resolution-related issues. Trey Research has recently entered into a joint venture with A. Datum Corporation. You must ensure that researchers from each organization can access data at the other company's site. Furthermore, you must ensure that sensitive documents are secured against being forwarded through email sent outside of the organization.

After completing this lab, you will be able to:

- Create a new Active Directory forest and domain.

- Configure name resolution for multiple Active Directory environments.

- Configure secondary zones and zone transfers.

- Install the Active Directory Rights Management Service role.

Estimated lesson time: 190 minutes

Project 12.1	Installing a New Active Directory Domain
Overview	To simulate the joint venture to a remote network, you must configure the A. Datum Corporation Active Directory environment in your test lab.
Outcomes	After completing this project, you will know how to: • Install a new Windows Server 2008 Active Directory forest and domain.
Completion time	30 minutes
Precautions	This exercise should only be performed on the even-numbered computer.

1. Press Ctrl+Alt+Delete on the even-numbered computer assigned to you and log on as the default administrator of the domain*xx*.local domain. Your username is Administrator. The password is MSPress#1 or the password that your instructor or lab proctor has assigned to you.

2. If the Server Manager console does not appear automatically, click Start, and then click Server Manager.

3. In the left pane, select Roles. In the right pane, click Add Roles.

4. Click Next to bypass the initial Welcome screen. The Select Server Roles screen is displayed.

5. Place a checkmark next to Active Directory Domain Services. Click Next. The Active Directory Domain Services screen is displayed.

6. Read the introductory information to Active Directory Domain Services and click Next. The Confirm Installation Selections screen is displayed.

7. Read the confirmation information to prepare for the installation. Click Install to install the Active Directory Domain Services role. The Installation Results screen is displayed.

8. Click Close This Wizard and launch the Active Directory Domain Services Installation Wizard (dcpromo.exe). The Welcome To The Active Directory Domain Services Installation Wizard screen is displayed.

9. Click Next twice to continue. The Choose A Deployment Configuration screen is displayed.

10. Click the Create A New Domain In A New Forest radio button. The Name The Forest Root Domain screen is displayed.

11. Key **domain*yy*.local** as the name of the new domain and click Next. The Set Forest Functional Level screen is displayed.

12. Select Windows Server 2008 and click Next. The Additional Domain Controller Options screen is displayed.

13. Verify that the DNS Server checkbox is selected, and then click Next. A warning message is displayed concerning DNS delegations.

14. Read the warning message and click Yes to continue. The *Location For Database, Log Files, And SYSVOL* screen is displayed.

15. Accept the default selections and click Next to continue. The Directory Services Restore Mode Administrator Password screen is displayed.

16. Key **MSPress#1** in the Password and Confirm Password text boxes, and click Next to continue. The Summary screen is displayed.

17. Review your installation choices and click Next to continue. The Active Directory Domain Services Installation Wizard screen is displayed, indicating that the Activie Directory Domain Service is being installed. The Completing The Active Directory Domain Services Installation Wizard screen is displayed.

18. Click Finish. When prompted, click Restart Now to restart the newly configured domain controller.

19. When the domain controller reboots, log onto the even-numbered computer as the default administrator of domain*yy*.local.

20. Verify that the even-numbered computer is configured to point only to itself for DNS name resolution. To verify, click Start and then click Control Panel. Double-click Network And Sharing Center. In the left pane, click Manage Network Connections. Right-click the Local Area Connection icon and click Properties. Select Internet Protocol Version 4 (TCP/IPv4) and click Properties. On the General tab, remove any DNS servers other than the loopback IP address (127.0.0.1) or the IP address of the RWDC*yy* server.

Project 12.2	Creating a Reverse Lookup Zone
Overview	You receive reports from your Help Desk manager stating that Help Desk analysts are having difficulties running certain TCP/IP troubleshooting utilities. Upon investigation, you realize that the DNS server for your domain is not configured with a reverse lookup zone for this subnet.
Outcomes	After completing this project, you will know how to: • Create a reverse lookup zone.
Completion time	20 minutes
Precautions	This exercise can be performed on either computer, even or odd.

1. Log on as the default administrator of the domain*zz*.local domain. Click the Start button, click Administrative Tools, and then click DNS.

2. Drill down to the Forward Lookup Zones node.

Question 1	*What forward lookup zones are present on your domain controller?*

3. Drill down to the Reverse Lookup Zones node.

Question 2	*What reverse lookup zones are present on your domain controller?*

4. To create a reverse lookup zone, right-click Reverse Lookup Zones in the left pane and click New Zone. The New Zone Wizard is displayed.

5. Click Next to bypass the initial Welcome screen. The Zone Type screen is displayed.

6. Click Primary Zone. Place a checkmark next to Store The Zone In Active Directory (this option is available only if DNS server is also a writeable domain controller) and click Next. The Active Directory Zone Replication Scope screen is displayed.

    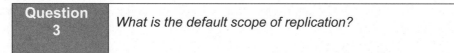

Question 3	*What is the default scope of replication?*

7. Accept the default selection and click Next. The Reverse Lookup Zone Name screen is displayed.

8. Select IPv4 Reverse Lookup Zone and click Next.

9. Enter the Network ID of your lab network; this value will be 192.168.1 or the value provided by your instructor or lab proctor. Click Next. The Dynamic Update screen is displayed.

Question 4	What is the default dynamic update setting?

10. Accept the default selection and click Next.

11. Click Finish. Confirm that the Reverse Lookup Zone is displayed in the DNS management console.

Project 12.3	Configuring Secondary Zones and Zone Transfers
Overview	As a part of the joint venture between Trey Research and A. Datum, Trey Research employees need to access servers on the A. Datum network, and vice versa. Management is concerned that name resolution for these servers will not be able to withstand an outage of a domain controller in either domain. You decide to configure a secondary zone on your local domain controller to host the DNS records pertaining to the remote domain.
Outcomes	After completing this project, you will know how to: • Configure DNS zone transfers. • Configure secondary DNS zones.
Completion time	30 minutes
Precautions	This exercise must be performed in pairs, on both the odd- and even-numbered computers.

■ PART A: Configure Zone Transfers

1. Log on as the default administrator of the domain*zz* domain.

2. Click the Start button, click Administrative Tools, and then click DNS.

3. Expand the Forward Lookup Zones node. Right-click the domain*zz*.local node and select Properties.

4. On the Zone Transfers tab, place a checkmark next to Allow Zone Transfers.

5. Select the Only To The Following Servers radio button and then click Edit.

6. In the IP addresses of the secondary servers section, click the Click Here To Add An IP Address Or Domain Name option, and then key the IP address of your partner's domain controller. For example, if you are working from RWDC01, enter the IP address of RWDC02, and vice versa. Press Enter and click OK.

> *Because this is a two-part process, you will see a red X in the Validated field, indicating that the server with this IP address is not authoritative for the required zone. You can safely disregard this error, because it will be resolved in Part B.*

■ Part B: Create a Secondary Zone

1. Right-click the Forward Lookup Zones node and select New Zone. Click Next to bypass the initial Welcome screen.

2. On the Zone Type screen, select a Secondary Zone and click Next. The Zone Name screen is displayed.

3. Enter the name of your partner's Active Directory domain. For example, if your domain name is *domain03.local*, key **domain04.local**. Click Next. The Master DNS Servers screen is displayed.

4. Enter the IP address of your partner's computer and press Enter. Confirm that a green checkmark is displayed next to the IP address and that the value of "OK" is displayed in the Validated column. Click Next. The Completing The Zone Wizard screen is displayed.

5. Click Finish. Expand the zone for your domain and confirm that an A record is displayed for your partner's domain controller.

Project 12.4	Installing the Rights Management Service Role
Overview	As a part of the joint venture between Trey Research and A. Datum Corporation, management has decided that sensitive documents need to be protected against accidental disclosure. To provide this protection, you decide to install the Active Directory Rights Management Service role on a domain controller within each domain.
Outcomes	After completing this project, you will know how to: • Install the Rights Management Service role.
Completion time	20 minutes
Precautions	You can perform this exercise on one or both computers.

■ PART A: Configuring a Service Account for the Active Directory Rights Management Service Role

1. Log onto the computer as the default administrator of the domain*zz*.local domain.

2. Click the Start button, key **cmd**, and then press Enter.

3. From the Windows command line, enter the following command: **dsadd user cn=RMSsvcacct,cn=users,dc=domain*zz*,dc=local –pwd MSPress#1**. Press Enter.

4. Key **exit** and press Enter to close the command-prompt window.

■ PART B: Install and Configure the Active Directory Rights Management Service Role

1. Log onto the computer as the default administrator of the domain*zz*.local domain.

2. If the Server Manager console does not appear automatically, click the Start button, and then click Server Manager.

3. In the left pane, select Roles. In the right pane, click Add Roles. Click Next to bypass the initial Welcome screen. The Select Server Roles screen is displayed.

4. Place a checkmark next to Active Directory Rights Management Service and click Next. The Add Roles Wizard screen is displayed, informing you that certain role services must be installed before you can install the RMS role.

5. Click Add Required Role Services and click Next. The Introduction To Active Directory Rights Management Services screen is displayed.

6. Read the information presented about the Active Directory Rights Management Service role, and then click Next. The Select Role Services screen is displayed.

7. Accept the default selection and click Next. The Create Or Join An AD RMS Cluster screen is displayed.

8. Notice that the Create A New RMS Cluster option is the only available option. Click Next to continue. The Select Configuration Database screen is displayed.

9. Select the Use Windows Internal Database On This Server radio button, and then click Next. The Specify Service Account screen is displayed.

10. Click Specify. The Windows Security window is displayed.

11. In the Windows Security window, enter the username and password of the account you created in Part A of this Project and click OK to close the window.

12. Click Next. The Configure AD RMS Cluster Key Storage screen is displayed.

13. Verify that the Use AD RMS Centrally Managed Key Storage radio button is selected and click Next. The Specify AD RMS Cluster Key Password screen is displayed.

14. Key **MSPress#1** in the Password and the Confirm Password fields, and then click Next. The Select AD RMS Cluster Web Site screen is displayed.

15. Verify that the Default Web Site is selected and then click Next. The Specify Cluster Address screen is displayed.

16. Select the Use An Unencrypted Connection (http://) radio button. (In a production AD RMS implementation, you should configure an SSL certificate on all AD RMS IIS Web servers; we are only selecting an http:// connection for the purposes of this exercise.)

17. Key **domain*zz*.local** in the Fully-Qualified Domain Name text box, and then click Validate. Click Next. The Name The Server Licensor Certificate screen is displayed. Verify that RWDC*zz* is entered into the Name text box, and then click Next. The Register AD RMS Service Connection Point screen is displayed.

18. Verify that the Register The AD RMS Service Connection Point Now radio button is selected, and then click Next. The Introduction To Web Server (IIS) screen is displayed.

19. Read the information displayed about the Internet Information Server (IIS), and then click Next. The Select Role Services screen is displayed.

20. Browse the role services that are selected for the IIS Web server role, and then click Next. The Confirm Installation Selections screen is displayed.

21. Click Install to begin the installation of the Active Directory Rights Management Service role. After the installation is complete, click Finish to close the Add Roles wizard.

LAB REVIEW QUESTIONS

Completion time	15 minutes

1. In your own words, describe what you learned by completing this lab.

2. Are Active Directory zone transfers configured for an entire DNS server or individual DNS zones?

3. When configuring zone transfers for a DNS zone, which options are available for you?

4. What is the difference between configuring a secondary zone for your partner's Active Directory domain versus configuring a forwarder for that domain? (Hint: Where are the DNS records stored?)

5. What command-line utility can you use to administer DNS zones and records on a Windows Server 2008 computer? (Hint: Use the Help and Support option to find a list of command-line utilities.)

LAB CHALLENGE 12.1	CREATING A CNAME RECORD
Overview	You wish to deploy several Web servers within your organization, and would like your Web developers to be able to use common aliases like www, www2, and www3 to access each Web server. To test the addition of multiple Web servers, you decide to create and test these three CNAME records for your domain controller to test name resolution.
Outcomes	After completing this exercise, you will know how to: • Create a CNAME record in Windows Server 2008 DNS.
Completion time	20 minutes
Precautions	If you do not perform the Lab Challenge, you must still perform the Post-Lab Cleanup.

POST-LAB CLEANUP	
Overview	Roll back all changes made in this lab.
Outcomes	After completing this project, you will know how to: • Decommission a Windows Server 2008 Active Directory domain. • Remove a secondary DNS zone. • Remove one or more installed server roles.
Completion time	30 minutes
Precautions	N/A

■ PART A: Decommission the Domain that was Created on the Even-Numbered Computer

1. On the even-numbered computer, log on as the default administrator of the domain*yy* domain.

2. Click Start, key **dcpromo,** and press Enter. The Active Directory Installation Wizard is displayed.

3. Click Next. An Active Directory Domain Services Installation Wizard warning is displayed, indicating that the server is a Global Catalog. Click OK. The *Remove Active Directory* page is displayed.

4. Place a checkmark next to Delete The Domain Because This Server Is The Last Domain Controller In The Domain, and press Next. If you receive a warning message indicating that this is the last DNS server for the reverse lookup zone for your subnet, click OK. The Application Directory Partitions screen is displayed, indicating that the DomainDNSZones and ForestDNSZones partitions will be deleted.

5. Click Next. The Confirm Deletion screen is displayed.

6. Place a checkmark next to Delete All Application Partitions On This Active Directory Domain Controller, and then click Next. The *Administrator Password* page is displayed.

7. Key **MSPress#1** in the New Administrator and Confirm Password text boxes. Click Next. The *Summary* page is displayed.

8. Confirm your selections. Click Next. The removal of Active Directory begins. This process will take several minutes. When the process is complete, the *Completing The Active Directory Installation Wizard* page is displayed.

9. Click Finish. The Active Directory Installation Wizard message appears, asking you to restart the computer.

10. Click Restart Now to complete the process.

11. When the computer reboots, log on using as the local Administrator of the RWDC*yy* computer. If the Server Manager console does not appear automatically, click the Start button, and then click Server Manager.

12. Drill down to the Roles node and click Remove Roles. Click Next to bypass the Welcome screen.

13. Remove the checkmark next to Active Directory Domain Services And DNS Server to remove these roles, and then click Next.

14. Click Remove to begin the removal process. Click Close when the removal process is complete. When prompted, reboot the RWDC*yy* server.

15. Reconfigure the DNS settings so that the RWDCyy computer points back to RWDC*xx* as its only DNS resolver, and then join RWDCyy to the domain*xx*.local domain as a member server.

■ PART B: Remove the Active Directory Rights Management Service and Associated Roles

1. Log onto each computer as the administrator of the domain*xx*.local domain.

2. If the Server Manager console does not appear automatically, click the Start button and then click Server Manager.

3. Drill down to the Roles node and click Remove Roles.

4. Click Next to bypass the *Welcome* screen. The *Remove Server Roles* screen is displayed.

5. Remove the checkmarks next to Active Directory Rights Management Services and Web Server (IIS). Click Next. The *Confirm Removal Selections* screen is displayed.

6. Click Remove to begin the removal process. The *Removal Results* screen is displayed.

7. Click Close and then click Yes to restart the server.

■ PART C: Final Cleanup

1. On the odd-numbered computer, log on as the administrator of the domain*xx*.local domain.

2. Delete the RMSsvcacct user account, as well as any records that were manually created in the domain*xx*.local Forward Lookup zone.

3. Delete the **domainyy.local** Forward Lookup zone and delete the Reverse Lookup Zone **1.168.192.in-addr.arpa**.

LAB 13
CONFIGURING ACTIVE DIRECTORY CERTIFICATE SERVICES

This lab contains the following projects and activities:

Project 13.1   Installing Active Directory Certificate Services

Project 13.2   Configuring Certificate Revocation

Project 13.3   Configuring Certificate Templates

Project 13.4   Configuring Certificate Enrollment

Project 13.5   Configuring Key Archival and Recovery

Lab Review Questions

Lab Challenge 13.1   Configuring EFS Certificates

Post-Lab Cleanup

BEFORE YOU BEGIN

Lab 13 assumes the following:

- The even-numbered computer must be configured to use the odd-numbered computer as its Preferred DNS Server, as described in Project 1.4.
- Active Directory is installed on the odd-numbered computer. Project 2.2 covers the installation of Active Directory on the odd-numbered computer.
- The even-numbered computer must be a member server within the odd-numbered computer's domain, as described in Project 7.1.

> *In this lab you will see the characters xx and yy. These directions assume that you are working on computers configured in pairs and that each computer has a number. One number is odd and the other number is even. For example, RWDC01 is the odd-numbered computer and RWDC02 is the even-numbered computer. When you see xx, substitute the unique number assigned to the odd-numbered computer. When you see yy, substitute the unique number assigned to the even-numbered computer.*

SCENARIO

You are a network administrator for Trey Research. The company uses a single Active Directory domain named treyresearch.net. The domain has a dozen Active Directory sites located throughout the United States. To increase security within the Trey Research network, you have decided to implement PKI certificates to allow secure communications with internal applications, such as intranet Web servers, as well as allowing users to encrypt sensitive files pertaining to government projects.

After completing this lab, you will be able to:

- Install and configure Active Directory Certificate Services.

- Configure enrollment and revocation of PKI certificates.

- Configure archival of PKI certificates.

Estimated lesson time: 190 minutes

> *Most of the exercises in this lab are performed on the even-numbered computer only. To gain the most exposure to working with Active Directory Certificate Services, students can take turns or work together when the lab requires work to be done on the even-numbered computer.*

Project 13.1	Installing Active Directory Certificate Services
Overview	To begin your deployment of Active Directory Certificate Services, you decide to deploy an enterprise root CA on a member server in your Active Directory domain.
Outcomes	After completing this project, you will know how to: • Install the Active Directory Certificate Services role on a Windows Server 2008 member server.
Completion time	30 minutes
Precautions	This exercise should only be performed on the even-numbered computer.

1. Press Ctrl+Alt+Delete on the even-numbered computer assigned to you and log on as the default administrator of the domain*xx*.local domain. Your username is Administrator. The password is MSPress#1 or the password that your instructor or lab proctor has assigned to you.

2. If the Server Manager console does not appear automatically, click Start, and then click Server Manager.

3. In the left pane, select Roles. In the right pane, click Add Roles.

4. Click Next to bypass the initial Welcome screen. The Select Server Roles screen is displayed.

5. Place a checkmark next to Active Directory Certificate Services. Click Next. The Active Directory Certificate Services screen is displayed.

6. Read the introductory information to Active Directory Certificate Services and click Next. The Select Role Services screen is displayed.

7. Place a checkmark next to the Certification Authority Role Service and click Next. The Specify Setup Type screen is displayed.

8. Select the Enterprise CA Type radio button and click Next. The Specify CA Type screen is displayed.

9. Select the Root CA Type radio button and click Next. The Set Up A Private Key screen is displayed.

10. Select the Create A New Private Key radio button and click Next. The Configure Cryptography For CA screen is displayed.

11. Accept the default values and click Next. The Configure CA Name screen is displayed.

Question 1	What is the common name configured for this CA by default?

12. Accept the default values and click Next. The Set Validity Period screen is displayed.

13. Accept the default value of 5 years and click Next. The Configure Certificate Database screen is displayed.

14. Accept the default values and click Next. The Confirm Installation Selections screen is displayed.

Question 2	What warning message do you see concerning the installation of the Active Directory Certificate Services role?

15. Read the confirmation information to prepare for the installation. Click Install to install the AD Certificate Services role. The Installation Results screen is displayed.

16. Click Close.

17. Log off of the even-numbered computer.

Project 13.2	Configuring Certificate Revocation
Overview	Before you can begin to deploy PKI certificates in a production environment, you need to configure certificate revocation so that your Active Directory Certificate Services infrastructure can react appropriately to certificates that need to be revoked because an employee resigns, an employee is terminated, or an employee's existing private key becomes stolen or otherwise compromised.
Outcomes	After completing this project, you will know how to: • Configure Certificate Revocation on an Active Directory Certificate Services server.
Completion time	30 minutes
Precautions	This exercise must be performed on the even-numbered computer.

■ PART A: Install the Online Responder

1. Log on to the even-numbered computer as the default administrator of the domain*xx*.local domain.

2. Click the Start button, and then click Server Manager. Drill down to Roles→Active Directory Certificate Services. Right-click Active Directory Certificate Services and select Add Role Services.

3. Place a checkmark next to Online Responder. The Add Role Services screen is displayed, indicating that you need to install several IIS components to install the Online Responder.

4. Click Add Required Role Services, and then click Next to continue. The Introduction To Web Server (IIS) screen is displayed.

5. Read the informational message concerning the installation of the Web Server role and click Next. The Select Role Services screen is displayed.

6. Accept the default IIS features to install and click Next. The Confirm Installation Selections screen is displayed.

7. Click Install to install the Online Responder role service. The Installation Progress screen is displayed. After a few minutes, the installation will complete.

8. Click Close when prompted.

■ PART B: Configure the Online Responder

1. In the left pane within Server Manager, drill down to Roles→Active Directory Certificate Services→Certificate Templates.

2. Right-click the OCSP Response Signing template and click Properties.

3. Click the Security tab. Click Add. The Select Users, Computers, Or Groups screen is displayed.

4. Click Object Types, place a checkmark next to Computers, and then click OK. Key **RWDCyy** and then click OK. Place a checkmark next to Enroll and Autoenroll under the Allow column, and then click OK.

5. In the left pane within Server Manager, drill down to Roles→Active Directory Certificate Services→DOMAINxx-RWDCyy-CA→Certificate Templates.

6. Right-click the Certificate Templates folder and click New→Certificate Template To Issue. Select the OCSP Response Signing certificate template and click OK.

■ PART C: Establish a Revocation Configuration for the Certification Authority

1. In the left pane of Server Manager, navigate to Roles→Active Directory Certificate Services→Online Responder: RWDCyy→Revocation Configuration.

2. Right-click Revocation Configuration and click Add Revocation Configuration. The Getting Started With Adding A Revocation Configuration screen is displayed.

3. Read the information on the Getting Started screen, and then click Next. The Name The Revocation Configuration screen is displayed.

4. Key **DOMAINxx-CA-REV** and click Next. The Select CA Certificate Location screen is displayed.

5. Verify that the Select A Certificate For An Existing Enterprise CA radio button is selected, and then click Next. The Choose CA Certificate screen is displayed.

6. Confirm that the Browse CA Certificates Published In Active Directory screen is selected, and then click Browse. The Select Certification Authority screen is displayed.

7. Verify that the DOMAINxx-RWDCyy-CA certificate is selected, and then click OK. Click Next to continue. The Select Signing Certificate screen is displayed.

8. Verify that the Automatically Select A Signing Certificate radio button is selected. Verify that a checkmark is next to Autoenroll For An OCSP Signing Certificate. Verify that the DOMAIN*xx*-RWDC*yy*-CA certificate is selected based on the OCSPResponseSigning template.

9. Click Next and then click Finish to configure the Revocation Configuration.

10. Navigate to DOMAIN*xx*-RWDC*yy*-CA→Issued Certificates. Verify that an OCSP Response Signing Certificate has been issued to the Certification Authority.

11. Log off of the even-numbered computer.

Project 13.3	Configuring Certificate Templates
Overview	Now that you have installed the Active Directory Certificate Services role and configured certificate revocation, you decide to deploy certificate templates that will allow user, computer, and Web server certificates to be deployed across your Active Directory network. Because your clients and servers are all running Windows XP, Windows Vista, Windows Server 2003, or Windows Server 2008, you wish to configure templates that allow certificate autoenrollment to ease the process of deploying certificates to your users and computers.
Outcomes	After completing this project, you will know how to: • Configure PKI certificate templates. • Publish certificate templates on a Windows Server 2008 CA.
Completion time	30 minutes
Precautions	This exercise must be performed on the even-numbered computer only.

■ PART A: Configure a Template for User Autoenrollment

1. Log onto the even-numbered computer as the default administrator of the domain*xx* domain.

2. Click Start, and then click Server Manager. In the left pane, drill down to Roles→Active Directory Certificate Services→Certificate Templates.

Question 3	*What is the minimum supported CA setting for the built-in User certificate template?*

3. To create a new certificate template to allow user autoenrollment, right-click the User template and click Duplicate Template. The Duplicate Template screen is displayed, prompting you for the minimum operating system version that should be supported by this template.

4. Select Windows Server 2008, Enterprise Edition, and then click OK. The Properties Of New Template window is displayed.

5. On the General tab, key **DOMAIN*xx*-User-Cert** in the Template Display Name text box. Confirm that a checkmark is next to the Publish Certificate In Active Directory option.

6. Click the Security tab. Click Domain Users, and then place a checkmark next to Read, Enroll, and Autoenroll.

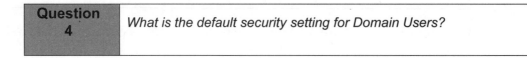

Question 4	What is the default security setting for Domain Users?

7. Click the Subject Name tab. Remove the checkmark next to Include E-mail Name In Subject Name. In the Include This Information In The Alternate Subject Name section, remove the checkmark next to E-mail Name.

8. Click the Superseded Templates tab. Click Add. The Add Superseded Templates screen is displayed.

9. Select the built-in User Certificate template, and then click OK.

10. Click OK.

■ PART B: Configure Computer and Web Server Certificate Templates

1. Right-click the Computer template and click Duplicate Template. The Duplicate Template screen is displayed, prompting you for the minimum operating system version that should be supported by this template.

2. Select Windows Server 2008, Enterprise Edition, and then click OK. The Properties Of New Template window is displayed.

3. On the General tab, key **DOMAIN*xx*-Computer-Cert** in the Template Display Name text box. Verify that a checkmark is next to the Publish Certificate In Active Directory option.

4 Click the Security tab. Click Domain Computers, and then place a checkmark next to Read, Enroll, and Autoenroll.

5. Click the Superseded Templates tab. Click Add. The Add Superseded Templates screen is displayed.

6. Select the built-in Computer Certificate template, and then click OK.

7. Click OK.

8. Right-click the Web server template and click Duplicate Template. The Duplicate Template screen is displayed, prompting you for the minimum operating system version that should be supported by this template.

9. Select Windows Server 2008, Enterprise Edition, and then click OK. The Properties Of New Template window is displayed.

10. On the General tab, key **DOMAIN*xx*-WebServer-Cert** in the Template Display Name text box. Verify that a checkmark is next to Publish Certificate In Active Directory.

11. Click the Security tab. Click Add. The Select Users, Computers, Or Groups screen is displayed.

12. Click Object Types, place a checkmark next to Computers, and then click OK. Key **RWDC*yy***, and then click OK. Place a checkmark next to Read, Enroll, and Autoenroll under the Allow column, and then click OK.

13. Click the Superseded Templates tab. Click Add. The Add Superseded Templates screen is displayed.

14. Select the built-in Web Server certificate template, and then click OK.

15. Click OK.

■ PART C: Configure the CA to Issue Certificates for Each Template

1. In the left pane, drill down to Roles→Active Directory Certificate Services→DOMAIN*xx*-RWDC*yy*-CA→Certificate Templates.

2. Right-click the Certificate Templates folder and click New→Certificate Template To Issue. The Enable Certificate Templates screen is displayed.

3. Click DOMAIN*xx*-User-Cert and click OK.

4. Repeat steps 2 and 3 to configure the CA to issue the DOMAIN*xx*-Computer-Cert and DOMAIN*xx*-WebServer-Cert certificate templates.

5. Log off of the even-numbered computer.

Project 13.4	Configuring Certificate Enrollment
Overview	You have determined that your Active Directory Certificate Services infrastructure is ready to be placed into production use on your network. To do this, you need to configure your user and computer accounts to allow PKI certificate autoenrollment. For those certificate types that do not allow autoenrollment, you need to use manual request mechanisms to obtain certificates for the appropriate users and computers.
Outcomes	After completing this project, you will know how to: • Configure Certificate Autoenrollment using Group Policy Objects. • Install the Certificate Services Web Enrollment service. • Request PKI certificates manually using the Certificate Services Web Enrollment service.
Completion time	30 minutes
Precautions	This exercise is presented in multiple parts. Part A is performed on the odd-numbered computer. The remaining parts are performed on the even-numbered computer.

■ PART A: Configure Certificate Autoenrollment for the DOMAIN*xx*.local Domain

1. Log on to the odd-computer as the default administrator of the domain*xx*.local domain.

2. Click the Start button, click Administrative Tools, and then click Group Policy Management.

3. Drill down to Forest: domain*xx*.local→Domains→Domain: domain*xx*.local→ Group Policy Objects→Default Domain Policy.

4. Right-click the Default Domain Policy, and then click Edit. The Group Policy Management Editor screen is displayed.

5. Drill down to the following node: User Configuration→Policies→Windows Settings→Security Settings→Public Key Policies. In the right pane, double-click Certificate Services Client – Auto-enrollment. The Certificate Services Client – Auto-enrollment Properties window is displayed.

6. In the Configuration model dropdown box, select Enabled. Place a checkmark next to the following items:

   a. Renew Expired Certificates, Update Pending Certificates, and Remove Revoked Certificates.

   b. Update Certificates That Use Certificate Templates.

7. Click OK.

8. Drill down to the following node: Computer Configuration→Policies→Windows Settings→Security Settings→Public Key Policies.

9. In the right pane, double-click Certificate Services Client – Auto-enrollment. The Certificate Services Client – Auto-enrollment Properties window is displayed.

10. In the Configuration model dropdown box, select Enabled. Place a checkmark next to the following items:

    a. Renew Expired Certificates, Update Pending Certificates, and Remove Revoked Certificates

    b. Update Certificates That Use Certificate Templates

11. Click OK, and then close the Group Policy Management Editor.

12. Open a command-prompt window and key **gpupdate /force**. Close the command-prompt window.

13. Reboot the even-numbered computer to force both user and computer autoenrollment to take place.

■ PART B: Install the Certification Authority Web Enrollment Role Service

1. Log on to the even-numbered computer as the default administrator of the domain*xx*.local domain.

2. Click the Start button, and then click Server Manager.

3. Drill down to Roles→Active Directory Certificate Services.

4. Right-click Active Directory Certificate Services and select Add Role Services.

5. Place a checkmark next to Certification Authority Web Enrollment. The Add Role Services screen is displayed, indicating that you need to install additional IIS components to install the Certification Authority Web Enrollment role service.

6. Click Add Required Role Services, and then click Next to continue. The Introduction To Web Server (IIS) screen is displayed.

7. Read the informational message concerning the installation of the Web Server role and click Next. The Select Role Services screen is displayed.

8. Accept the default IIS features to install and click Next. The Confirm Installation Selections screen is displayed.

9. Click Install to install the Certification Authority Web Enrollment role service. The Installation Progress screen is displayed. After a few minutes, the installation will complete.

10. Click Close when prompted.

■ PART C: Request a Web Server Certificate for the Even-Numbered Computer

1. Click the Start button, click Administrative Tools, and then click Internet Information Services (IIS) Manager. The Internet Information Services (IIS) Manager page will be displayed.

2. In the left pane, double-click the RWDC*yy* node. The RWDC*yy* Home screen will be displayed in the main pane.

3. Scroll down to the IIS section and double-click the Server Certificates icon. In the right pane, click Create Domain Certificate. The Distinguished Name Properties screen is displayed.

4. Enter the following information and then click Next. The Online Certification Authority screen is displayed.

    a. Common name: rwdc*yy*.domain*xx*.local

    b. Organization: DOMAIN*xx*.LOCAL

    c. Organizational Unit: HQ

    d. City/Locality: Redmond

    e. State/province: WA

    f. Country/region: US

5. Click Select next to the Specify Online Certification Authority text box. The Select Certification Authority screen is displayed.

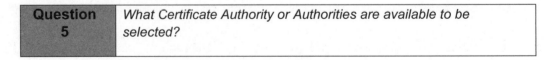

Question 5	What Certificate Authority or Authorities are available to be selected?

6. Click DOMAIN*xx*-RWDC*yy*-CA and click OK. In the Friendly Name text box, key **rwdc*yy*.domain*xx*.local** and click Finish.

■ PART D: Enable SSL Connections on the Even-Numbered Computer

1.   In the left pane of the IIS Manager, expand the Sites node.

2.   Right-click Default Web Site and click Edit Bindings. The Site Bindings screen is displayed.

3.   Click Add. The Add Site Binding screen is displayed.

4.   In the Type dropdown box, select https. In the SSL Certificate dropdown box, select rwdc*yy*.domain*xx*.local.

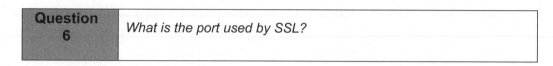

Question 6	*What is the port used by SSL?*

5.   Click OK and then click Close.

6.   In the left pane of IIS Manager, drill down to the Default Web Site→CertSrv node. Double-click CertSrv. In the main pane, double-click SSL Settings.

7.   Place a checkmark next to Require SSL, and then click Apply in the Action pane.

8.   Log off of the even-numbered computer.

Project 13.5	Configuring Key Archival and Recovery
Overview	Management is concerned about users losing the private keys associated with their PKI certificates. After consulting with management and key members of the Trey Research staff, you determine that it will not be sufficient to simply instruct users to back up their private keys on an individual basis. Accordingly, you decide to configure key archival on your Certificate Services server to enable administrators to recover private keys that become lost or otherwise unavailable.
Outcomes	After completing this project, you will know how to: • Configure key archival on an Active Directory Certificate Services server. • Establish one or more users as key recovery agents within an Active Directory domain.
Completion time	30 minutes
Precautions	This exercise is presented in multiple parts. Part A is performed on the odd-numbered computer. The remaining parts are performed on the even-numbered computer.

■ PART A: Create a User Account to Act as a Key Recovery Agent

1. Log on to the odd-numbered computer as the default administrator of the domain*xx*.local domain.

2. Create a user account in the Users container called RECOVERY with a password of MSPress#1. The RECOVERY account only needs to be a member of the Domain Users group.

3. Log off of the odd-numbered computer.

■ PART B: Configure a Key Recovery Agent Certificate Template

1. Log on to the even-numbered computer as the default administrator of the domain*xx*.local domain.

2. In the left pane of the Server Manager console, browse to Roles→Active Directory Certificate Services→Certificate Templates.

3. Right-click the Key Recovery Agent template and select Properties. On the General tab, place a checkmark next to Publish Certificate In Active Directory.

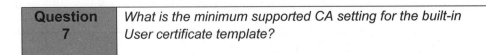

Question 7	What is the minimum supported CA setting for the built-in User certificate template?

4. Click the Security tab. Click Add. The Select Users, Computers, Or Groups screen is displayed.

5. Key **RECOVERY** and click OK. Under the Allow column, place a checkmark next to Read and Enroll. Click OK.

6. In the left pane, expand the DOMAIN*xx*-RWDC*yy*-CA node. Right-click Certificate Templates and click New→Certificate Template To Issue.

7. Select the Key Recovery Agent template and click OK.

8. Log off of the even-numbered computer.

■ PART C: Request a Key Recovery Agent Certificate

1. Log on to the even-numbered computer as the default administrator of the domain*xx*.local domain.

2. In the Security Information section of the Server Manager console, click Configure IE ESC. The Internet Explorer Enhanced Security Configuration screen is displayed.

3. Under the Administrators section, click Off and then click OK.

4. Open an Internet Explorer browser window. Key the following URL: **https://rwdc*yy*.domain*xx*.local/certsrv**. The Connect To rwdc*yy*.domain*xx*.local window is displayed.

5. Key **DOMAIN*xx*\RECOVERY** as the username, key **MSPress#1** as the password, and then click OK. If you are prompted to enable the Microsoft Phishing Filter, click Turn On Automatic Phishing Filter (Recommended) and click OK. The Welcome page is displayed.

6. Click Request A Certificate. The Request A Certificate page is displayed.

7. Click Submit An Advanced Certificate Request. The Advanced Certificate Request page is displayed.

8. Click Create and submit a request to this CA. If the Information Bar is displayed, prompting you to install the Certificate Enrollment ActiveX Control, run the control when prompted. The Advanced Certificate Request page is displayed again.

9. In the Certificate Template dropdown menu, select Key Recovery Agent. Click Submit. A warning message is displayed, indicating that the Web site is requesting a certificate on your behalf.

10. Click Yes to continue. The Certificate pending window is displayed. Make a note of the Request ID for use in the next section.

11. Close Internet Explorer.

■ PART D: Approve the Key Recovery Agent Certificate Request

1. In the left pane of the Server Manager console, browse to Roles→Active Directory Certificate Services→DOMAIN*xx*-RWDC*yy*-CA→Pending Requests. You will see the pending certificate request created in Part C.

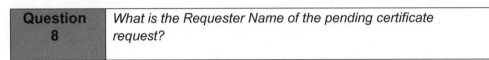

Question 8	What is the Requester Name of the pending certificate request?

2. Right-click the certificate request and click All Tasks→Issue.

3. Verify that the certificate is displayed in the Issued Certificates node.

■ PART E: Retrieve the Approved Key Recovery Agent Certificate

1. Open an Internet Explorer browser window. Enter the following URL: **https://rwdc*yy*.domain*xx*.local/certsrv**. The Connect To rwdc*yy*.domain*xx*.local window is displayed.

2. Key **DOMAIN*xx*\RECOVERY** as the username, key **MSPress#1** as the password, and then click OK. The Welcome page is displayed.

3. Click View The Status Of A Pending Certificate Request. The View The Status Of A Pending Certificate Request page is displayed.

4. Click the pending certificate request. The Certificate Issued screen is displayed.

5. Click Install This Certificate. A warning message is displayed, asking you to confirm that one or more certificates should be installed from this Website onto the local computer.

6. Click Yes to continue. The Certificate Installed screen is displayed, indicating that the certificate has been installed successfully.

7. Close the Internet Explorer window.

■ PART F: Configure a Certificate Template with a Key Recovery Agent

1. In the left pane of the Server Manager console, browse to Roles→Active Directory Certificate Services→DOMAIN*xx*-RWDC*yy*-CA. Right-click DOMAIN*xx*-RWDC*yy*-CA and click Properties. The DOMAIN*xx*-RWDC*yy*-CA Properties page is displayed.

2. Click the Recovery Agents tab. Select the Archive The Key radio button and verify that the Number Of Recovery Agents To Use is set to 1.

3. Click Add. The Key Recovery Agent selection screen is displayed.

4. Verify that the Key Recovery Agent certificate for the RECOVERY user account is selected, and then click OK.

5. Click OK. You will be prompted to restart Active Directory Certificate Services. Click Yes to continue.

6. In the left pane, browse to Roles→Active Directory Certificate Services→Certificate Templates.

7. Right-click the DOMAIN*xx*-User-Cert template and click Properties. Click the Request Handling tab.

8. Place a checkmark next to the Archive Subject's Encryption Private Key option and the Use Advanced Symmetric Algorithm To Send The Key To The CA option, and then click OK.

9. Log off of the even-numbered computer.

LAB REVIEW QUESTIONS

Completion time	15 minutes

1. In your own words, describe what you learned by completing this lab.

2. Will the configuration that you established in this lab allow you to take your root CA offline for added security? Why or why not?

3. Why did you need to create copies of the User and Computer templates during this lab?

4. Does a key recovery agent require any special permissions within Active Directory, such as Domain Admin or Server Operator group membership?

5. What command-line utility can you use to administer PKI certificates on a Windows Server 2008 computer? (Hint: Use the Help and Support option to find a list of command-line utilities.)

LAB CHALLENGE 13.1	CONFIGURING EFS CERTIFICATES
Overview	Trey Research has recently won several government research contracts that require limited access to sensitive files. To provide an additional layer of security for these files, you wish to configure PKI certificates to allow users working on these projects to encrypt their files.
Outcomes	After completing this exercise, you will know how to: • Configure EFS certificate templates. • Enroll the RECOVERY user for an EFS certificate.
Completion time	20 minutes
Precautions	If you do not perform the Lab Challenge, you must still perform the Post-Lab Cleanup to prepare the lab environment for Troubleshooting Lab C.

POST-LAB CLEANUP	
Overview	Roll back all changes made in this lab and prepare for the final troubleshooting lab.
Outcomes	After completing this project, you will know how to: • Decommission a Windows Server 2008 Certificate Services server. • Install an Active Directory forest root domain.
Completion time	30 minutes
Precautions	N/A

■ PART A: Decommission the Certificate Services Server

1. On the even-numbered computer, log on as the default administrator of the domain*xx* domain. If the Server Manager console is not displayed automatically, click the Start button, and then click Server Manager.

2. Drill down to the Roles node and click Remove Roles.

3. Click Next to bypass the Welcome screen. The Remove Server Roles screen is displayed.

4. Remove the checkmarks next to Active Directory Certificate Services and Web Server (IIS). Click Next. The Confirm Removal Selections screen is displayed.

5. Click Remove to begin the removal process. The Removal Results screen is displayed.

6. Click Close, and then click Yes to restart the server.

■ PART B: Configure the Even-Numbered Computer as a Separate Domain

1. In the left pane of Server Manager, select Roles. In the right pane, click Add Roles.

2. Click Next to bypass the initial Welcome screen. The Select Server Roles screen is displayed.

3. Place a checkmark next to Active Directory Domain Services. Click Next. The Active Directory Domain Services screen is displayed.

4. Read the introductory information to Active Directory Domain Services and click Next. The Confirm Installation Selections screen is displayed.

5. Read the confirmation information to prepare for the installation. Click Install to install the Active Directory Domain Services role. The Installation Results screen is displayed.

6. Click Close This Wizard And Launch The Active Directory Domain Services Installation Wizard (dcpromo.exe). The Welcome to the Active Directory Domain Services Installation Wizard screen is displayed.

7. Click Next twice to continue. The Choose A Deployment Configuration screen is displayed.

8. Click the Create A New Domain In A New Forest radio button. The Name the Forest Root domain screen is displayed.

9. Enter **domain*yy*.local** as the name of the new domain and click Next. The Set Forest Functional Level screen is displayed.

10. Select Windows Server 2008 and click Next. The Additional Domain Controller Options screen is displayed.

11. Verify that the DNS Server checkbox is selected, and then click Next. A warning message is displayed concerning DNS delegations.

12. Read the warning message and click Yes to continue. The Location For Database, Log Files, And SYSVOL screen is displayed.

13. Accept the default selections and click Next to continue. The Directory Services Restore Mode Administrator Password screen is displayed.

14. Key **MSPress#1** in the Password: and Confirm Password: text boxes. Click Next to continue. The Summary screen is displayed.

15. Review your installation choices and click Next to continue. The Active Directory Domain Services Installation Wizard screen is displayed, indicating that the Active Directory Domain Services service is being installed. The Completing The Active Directory Domain Services Installation Wizard is displayed.

16. Click Finish. When prompted, click Restart Now to restart the newly configured domain controller.

17. When the domain controller reboots, log on to the even-numbered computer as the default administrator of domain*yy*.local.

18. Verify that the even-numbered computer is configured to point only to itself for DNS name resolution. To verify, click Start→Control Panel. Double-click Network And Sharing Center.

19. In the left pane, click Manage Network Connections. Right-click the Local Area Connection icon and click Properties. Select Internet Protocol Version 4 (TCP/IPv4) and click Properties. On the General tab, remove any DNS servers other than the loopback IP address (127.0.0.1) or the IP address of the RWDC*yy* server.

■ PART C: FINAL CLEANUP

1. On the odd-numbered computer, log on as the administrator of the domain*xx*.local domain.

2. Delete the key recovery agent user account.

LAB C
TROUBLESHOOTING

BEFORE YOU BEGIN

Troubleshooting Lab C is a practical application of the knowledge you have acquired from Lessons 9 through 13. Troubleshooting Lab C is divided into two sections: "Reviewing a Network" and "Troubleshooting a Break Scenario." In the "Reviewing a Network" section, you will review and assess a Windows Server 2008 Active Directory infrastructure for Litware, Inc. In the "Troubleshooting a Break Scenario" section, you will troubleshoot a break scenario. Your instructor or lab assistant has changed your computer configuration, causing it to "break." Your task in this section will be to apply your acquired skills to troubleshoot and resolve the break.

REVIEWING A NETWORK

You are a computer consultant. Amy Rusko, the chief information officer of Litware, Inc., has hired you to help her address several security concerns. The Litware network consists of two Active Directory domains: litwareinc.com and dev.litwareinc.com. The litwareinc.com domain consists of six Windows Server 2008 domain controllers and nine member servers, some running Windows Server 2003 and some running Windows Server 2008. The company has 1,300 employees with user accounts in the litwareinc.com domain, and each employee has a desktop computer running Windows Vista Business.

The child domain, dev.litwareinc.com, is where the accounts and resources for employees involved in research, engineering, and support reside. This domain consists of 4 Windows Server 2008 domain controllers, 6 Windows Server 2003 member servers, and 300 client machines running Windows Vista Business. The member servers include three application servers and three file servers. The file servers contain large amounts of data, including many confidential development documents containing trade secrets regarding new toys.

Amy has identified two areas of concern related to security:

- It was recently discovered that one of the company's top designers had been forwarding confidential information to a competitor in an attempt to secure a position there. Amy wants to find a way to prevent any other company designers from printing sensitive documents or forwarding them outside of the company.

- Amy wants to be able to track users who access or attempt to access documents stored on three file servers that contain confidential information. She plans to keep a log of all this information and never wants to miss any successful or unsuccessful attempt to access this data.

Given Amy's security concerns, answer the following questions:

1. What can the company deploy to control access to sensitive documents?

2. How can access and attempted access to the folders containing Litware's confidential documents be tracked?

3. Where will a record of access attempts to sensitive documents be stored?

4. Amy wants to ensure that records of access to sensitive documents are retained for at least 14 days so that they can be reviewed by auditors and management. How can you easily ensure that all Litware servers adhere to this requirement?

5. Amy tells you that a domain administrator accidentally deleted hundreds of user and computer accounts within an Active Directory OU. The change replicated throughout the domain. She says that it took nearly a day to re-create the deleted objects. What can you suggest to prevent this problem from happening in the future?

TROUBLESHOOTING A BREAK SCENARIO

In this portion of Troubleshooting Lab C, you must resolve a "break" scenario that has been introduced by your instructor or lab assistant.

NOTE	*Do not proceed with break instructions until you receive guidance from your instructor. Your instructor or lab assistant will inform you which break scenario you will be performing (Break Scenario 1 or Break Scenario 2) and which computer to use. Your instructor or lab assistant might also have special instructions. Consult with your instructor or lab assistant before proceeding.*

Break Scenario 1

You are a domain administrator for Litware, Inc. A desktop administrator reports some peculiar behavior with four user accounts. Users are not supposed to have the Run menu option on their Start menus, but three of four newly created user accounts have it. The desktop administrator is puzzled. Fill out Table C-1 for each new user account in the left column. In the right column, explain why each user does or does not have the Run menu. All user accounts use MSPRess#1 as their password and are on the domain*xx* domain.

Table C-1
User Accounts and the Run Option

User account	*Is Run on the Start menu? If so, why?*
LynnLC	
RobertLC	
LauraLC	
LindaLC	

As you resolve this configuration issue, record the following information:

- A description of the issue

- A list of all steps taken to diagnose the problem, even those that did not work

- A description of the problem

- A description of the solution

- A list of the tools and resources used to solve this problem

Break Scenario 2

You are the network administrator at Litware, Inc. A user named Yan Li needs to complete a report for her manager, but her workstation has failed and it is currently unrecoverable. You want to let her use your domain controller to finish writing the report. She tries to log on but fails. Yan Li's username is Yan, and her password is MSPress#1. You must find a way for her to be able to log on locally to the domain controller.

Allowing normal users to log on locally to domain controllers is not a security best practice; we are allowing this here as an exercise in Group Policy troubleshooting only.

As you resolve this configuration issue, record the following information:

- A description of the issue

- A list of all steps taken to diagnose the problem, even those that did not work

- A description of the problem

- A description of the solution

- A list of the tools and resources used to solve this problem